WHAT PEOPLE ARE SAYING ABOUT
FINDING THE MISSING PEACE

"Chris Duffy-Wentzel's journey of healing physically, emotionally and spiritually is fascinating. Her journey is so compelling that I could not stop reading her book. Her honesty touched my heart. Her humor made me laugh out loud. She tells her life story with an open heart as she recounts her insights and lessons in life."

—**Peggy Huddleston** Author, *Prepare for Surgery, Heal Faster: A Guide of Mind-Body Techniques*

"*Finding the Missing Peace* has a universal appeal. The element of mystery in it will engage the heart of the reader who will journey right with the author. The book is a life-giving gift that will help others in their search for healing."

—**Beth Kingsley Hawkins**, M. A., music psychotherapist

"*Finding the Missing Peace* is both a compelling mystery and a spiritual search for a deeper identity. It is a captivating, uplifting, and heart-opening story of Chris Duffy-Wentzel's search for her birth mother. Once I began reading her book, I did not want to put it down as I followed Chris along the path of unravelling the mystery of her birth. I read in wonder as she uncovered essential clues through unconventional psychic means when adoption agencies refused to help her, and how in the process of this search, she found something very precious—a deep sense of her own identity and her true spiritual essence."

—**Marjorie Woollacott PhD**, Neuroscientist and Author, *Infinite Awareness: The Awakening of a Scientific Mind*

"Numerous times during reading this heart-warming story I was inspired and moved to tears. At every turn, the courage, eager openness to learning the truth and tenacity of the author-as-detective never disappoints. The story, as if woven by magic, left me with a deeper and more expanded understanding of the power and importance of mother."

—**Susanne Bennett**, Editor, Public Speaker, Personal Coach

"We all have a journey but few have the depth of soul and open mind to follow the path through time and space the way Chris Duffy-Wentzel has. Relish her story and perhaps let her guide your heart along your own winding road".

—**MJ Proske**, Yoga Instructor, Author

"Chris's life story is truly a journey shared with unconditional love. A compelling read that kept me turning pages for the next sequel to unfold. Her journey of healing takes the reader through the struggle of a linear-led life to the empowered connection to Spirit leading her to all that she asked for and needed in her life. Chris's authenticity and integrity to share the truth about her past is truly inspirational."

—**Rev. Michelle Love**, Medium, Psychic and founder of Light the Way, Naples, Florida

"I applaud Chris Duffy-Wentzel for bravely facing the barriers as she walked the maze of seeking her family identity and putting the puzzle together in-spite of the many barriers she faced. She persevered and has come out finding her sense of balance so she can look to the future feeling rooted so she can have a joyful outlook towards the future."

—**Grandmother Mona Polacca**, of The International Council of 13 Indigenous Grandmothers. Hopi/Havasupai and Tewa. Featured in the books: *For the Next 7 Generations and GRANDMOTHERS WISDOM: Reverence for All Creation*

"Chris Duffy-Wentzel has written an absolutely compelling story of her 30-year search for her biological parents, spurred by her need to obtain her critical medical history before surgery. Her story includes fascinating details of her adoptive parents' journey, as well as clever detective work that led her to answers she was seeking. She opened her search to many avenues, even including startling revelations from a psychic, as well as receiving guidance from her ancestors, using techniques she learned in a lifetime of spiritual seeking."

—**Bill Worth**, author of the novels *House of the Sun: A Metaphysical Novel of Maui; The Hidden Life of Jesus Christ: A Memoir;* plus the non-fiction book, *Outwitting Multiple Sclerosis: How I Healed My Brain By Changing My Mind*

FINDING THE MISSING PEACE

A HEALING JOURNEY TO WHOLENESS

CHRIS DUFFY-WENTZEL

Ancestor Hill Press
Cornville, Arizona
www.kachinawoman.com

Printed in the United Sates

2021903189

Library of Congress Cataloging-in-Publication Data

ISBN: 978-1-64184-540-3 (Paperback)
ISBN: 978-1-64184-541-0 (Ebook)

Cover photographs taken by June Rettinger de Arballo on Oak Creek at Cathedral Rock, a powerful vortex in Sedona, Arizona.

Cover design by Marcus Badgley

AUTHOR'S NOTE

This is the story of my life. Most of the memories are my own, as well as the memories of my parents, aunts and family friends. I've done my best with the timeline accuracy and re-creation of the dialogue, confirming when possible. Given the nature of the story some names have been changed to ensure privacy.

To my ancestors and guides on the other side who nudged, encouraged, and ultimately demanded I share our healing story.

CONTENT

FOREWORD

On a wintry weekend morning in mid-January, I was in my living room unpacking the last bits of furnishings after a recent move back to New England. Suddenly, I felt a subtle wind inside the room. This whisper wind carried a message guiding me to retrieve a set of chimes given to me by Chris, a friend and former colleague whom I hadn't seen in six years.

The message sounded in my heart and told me to retrieve the chimes and hang them. I knew I would be hearing from Chris soon. The feeling tone of the message conveyed that the coming interaction was important. I understood I was being called to be a part of whatever was unfolding in Chris's life.

I located the chimes and hung them in front of a northwest-facing window on the second floor where I could hear the uplifting sparkle of their high notes as I settled into my new home. Several days later, I received a phone call from Chris.

Life summons and speaks to us in many ways. We can experience multiple forms of knowing and communication with Spirit when we recognize and allow it. Some messages demand immediate attention, others are significant for a period of our lives, and others may be significant for an entire lifetime. On occasion, we receive messages that are eternal in nature and transcend any single life. The message that came to me on the wind that day had the initial feeling of being significant for a single life but would turn out to have an eternal message imbedded in it.

On the day Chris called, she shared a recent cancer diagnosis. In her voice I heard bewilderment, fear, and determination. When she asked for my help, the message of the spirit wind was confirmed. I knew I was meant to participate in Chris's journey.

I had graduated from medical school and became licensed as a Naturopathic Doctor and Acupuncturist. Prior to that, I spent many years training in energy healing, energy diagnosis, and meditation. I understood I was being called into service in a way that would require me to utilize all my training in whatever form needed. Most importantly, in this work I would be connecting with direct guidance from Spirit.

To heal on all levels, we must be open to what is true within us. Even though I had extensive training, I would not always know the answers, the direction, or the pace and sequencing of Chris's healing journey. It wasn't for me to determine the route or outcome, nor to eliminate any avenue of healing that might be helpful, including conventional medical methods. Answers are not always found in books, from the teachings we have been given, nor the expertise we may have gained. Instead, they are found deep within. The guidance needed arrived through an open connection to a higher order of wisdom, love, and healing, not only in my participation but, necessarily, from within Chris.

Chris's cancer diagnosis became a catalyst for profound changes in her life. As her deepening into her spiritual journey evolved, she experienced an awakening which asked her to embrace an idea new to her: healing was not about fixing anything that was broken. This was the eternal message that transcended her individual life. Amidst her determination,

INTRODUCTION

It was a perfect fall day, 2009. The sun shone brightly on the legendary fall colors of Upstate New York, the sky an intense blue. I was excited for a long-awaited weekend Wellness Retreat. The phone rang as I left the yoga studio and the perfect day turned into a nightmare. In an instant my life turned upside down, as the news, "You have uterine cancer. Schedule a surgical consult immediately," took hold.

Suddenly, I found myself confronted with a gut-wrenching decision that impacted people beyond my immediate family. A three-decade search for my birth mother – one that I had given my word years earlier to stop – would need to be reignited. The extent of the surgery and my quality-of-life post-surgery was directly linked to knowing my birth mother's medical history.

I was in a race against time to unlock the secrets trapped within my sealed adoption records.

Past attempts using traditional search methods and playing by the Adoption Agency's rules had failed. Becoming my own "Adoption Detective" would be key in solving a lifelong mystery.

Through this spiritual detective work I found myself on an unexpected adventure that challenged my scientific beliefs, and led me to a medical medium, an astrologer, a psychic, and past-life regression therapy.

Finding answers in different places – beyond science and reason – placed me on a unique path, which eventually led to an integrated healing journey focused on my physical, emotional, and spiritual wellbeing.

Was it possible to change long-held beliefs, solve the adoption puzzle and heal cancer without surgery? The answer was clear: I needed to feel in order to heal. As a workaholic perfectionist who had mastered the art of busyness to avoid painful emotions, this was terrifying.

My cancer diagnosis became the catalyst for profound life changes. The unexpected journey evolved into much more than finding missing pieces of the past. A peace arose that did not depend on the unpredictable nature of outside forces. **Cancer healed me!**

Finding the Missing Peace shares the process and resources I used to embrace the idea that healing is not about fixing anything that's broken. It's about self-acceptance, unlocking your unique greatness and remembering the wholeness that is you.

This is my heartfelt intention for every reader.

– Offered with love and many blessings,

Chris Duffy-Wentzel

1

A RACE AGAINST TIME

"Empowerment is realizing you are the one who needs to say the things you've waited your entire life to hear."

—**Matt Kahn**

"Is this Chris?" she began. Instantly, a sick feeling washed over me. I managed to take a long, deep breath, as I prepared for the call I had been anticipating for weeks.

"This is Monica from Dr. Heath's office. Your lab results are back from pathology. The cells are abnormal and the doctor would like you to schedule a D and C as soon as possible for additional information." I felt a wave of fear and anxiety wash over me as I tried to find my calm voice. I assured her I would consult my work schedule and make the appointment. I didn't have to ask technical or medical questions, as I fully grasped what she had said. I had spent my career as an immuno-virologist, and now, a senior director in a Medical Device organization that specialized in women's health care. I knew a lot about breast, cervical, and uterine health, and the impact a cancer diagnosis would have on my quality of life, or even my life itself. At this point, I was wishing I didn't have to experience my professional work so "up close and personal." I put my phone away, surprised to see that nothing looked different from how it looked just moments ago, before Monica's call. The sunlight was still illuminating the changing fall leaves and the air felt clean and crisp against my face. Yet I knew, deep inside, everything about my life was going to change. The first domino had tipped. As I boarded the shuttle bus to take me to the yoga center, it dawned on me that it was fortuitous that months earlier I had enrolled in a yoga and meditation workshop in Upstate New York. This was part of my ongoing quest to live a healthier, more balanced life. *Great. Nothing like a potential life-threatening diagnosis to force the application of the things I was there to learn and practice.*

My mind was flooded with "what if" scenarios, one more frightening than the other. Isn't it funny how the mind never brings in all the potential positive outcomes? Nope … just the kind of thoughts that scare the living **** out of you! Somehow, the phrase, "Be present and know you are okay in this moment," managed to make its way through the fear clouding my mind. I was about to encounter numerous opportunities to "practice being in the moment," a cornerstone principle from spiritual teacher and author, Eckhart Tolle. A friend had given me a copy of his book, *The Power of Now,* and at this moment I was feeling very grateful to have discovered tools that would help me as I waited for the D and C procedure.

Just breathe. You are okay right now. You're sitting on a bus in Upstate New York. Okay, so far so good. Tension is leaving my body and the fear is dissolving. This is working! Whoops. Not so fast; my mind raced ahead, conjuring worst-case scenarios. Then seconds later ... *you're making progress just by being AWARE of your thoughts.*

Thankfully, something my yoga teacher said helped put me out of my self-imposed misery: "Coming back to the breath as often as you need to, without judgment, will cool the agitation of the mind." I would discover many humble reminders that weekend of why yoga is referred to as a "practice."

My team's biggest training event of the year was fast approaching, and I scheduled the D&C procedure for immediately afterwards. The only person I told was my husband, Dave, still my best friend, years after our meeting in high school. For a time, I managed to keep my fears at bay with my hectic work schedule. The results of the second call from my OBGYN would force me to now confront the truth.

"The pathologist report confirms uterine cancer. Please schedule a consult with the surgeon in Boston." I met with a highly recommended female surgeon from one of the top cancer hospitals in Boston. She was very upbeat and positive. "It is early stage, and in instances like this, we won't leave anything to chance that could cause a problem down the road." Her recommendation was a total hysterectomy, including the removal of my ovaries. She added that based on my age and menopausal status, "I didn't need them anyway." For extra convincing, she said, "This is THE most common surgery I perform in women your age." I realized she was trying to reassure me. It had the opposite effect, as alarm bells went off in my head. I recalled cases I had seen working in the laboratory. *Why is that? Is she over diagnosing and over treating? I'm in late-stage menopause and my hormones are crazy right now. Is it possible the cells are abnormal as they're transitioning? I recalled recently hearing* about a work colleague who had a similar diagnosis. Upon completing a total hysterectomy, the subsequent pathology report from the lab showed NO cancer detected. She suffered emotionally and physically for years afterwards. That certainly wasn't a path I wanted to take.

Despite my questions and doubts, I conceded that the surgeon had seen way more cases than I had. The safe thing for me to do was to follow her advice, resolve this quickly and "get back to my life." I scheduled the operation for over the Christmas holidays, to minimize my time out of work.

On the drive home, the real reason behind my unsettled feelings surfaced. I found myself confronted with a gut-wrenching decision that impacted people beyond my immediate family. A three-decade search for my birth mother—one that I had given my word years earlier to stop—would need to be re-ignited. The extent of the surgery and my quality-of-life post-surgery was directly linked to knowing my birth mother's medical history. I was in a race against time to unlock the secrets trapped within my sealed adoption records. Past attempts using traditional search methods and playing by the Adoption Agency's rules had failed. Becoming my own "Adoption Detective would be key in solving a lifelong mystery. My life depended on it.

Tears of frustration and uncertainty streamed down my face as I pulled into my driveway. "**This changes everything!**" I shouted to whomever was listening.

2

HOPE AND DETERMINATION

*"I learned that courage is not the absence of fear
but the TRIUMPH over it."*

—**Nelson Mandela**

L ater that evening, needing a distraction from the decision weighing heavily on my mind, I pulled an old family photo album from the book case. Paging through it, a particular picture of Trudy, my adoptive mother, and me caught my attention. It reminded me of how my medical diagnosis and treatment were similar to her situation. Although, she would face her life-altering decision at a much earlier age.

Trudy was in her late twenties, and about to be married. Excitement was replaced by despair as she was told heartbreaking news by her doctor a few months before her wedding. Devastated, she wondered how she could move forward with plans to marry and start a family. Sharing her situation with her two sisters, they reminded her of all she had survived in her young life. The next morning, she awoke with a plan and a promise. Afterall, she had survived the Depression, near-fatal blood poisoning, ridicule, and prejudice. She would find a way. Trudy's strict German parents escaped Germany as WW1 was intensifying. They wanted to ensure their children would have a better life in America.

Trudy's father had been a successful inventor and businessman, patenting a revolutionary prosthetic device for soldiers who had lost limbs. They left behind all their possessions, and much of their wealth, to come to Ellis Island in New York. Gertrude Olga Thurman (Trudy to her friends) was born in Elizabeth, New Jersey, a city just over the bridge from New York City. It was filled with immigrants who had also arrived on Ellis Island with big dreams for a better life. Her mother, Matilda, helped support the family as a seamstress as her father, Emil struggled to start a business at a time when there was great suspicion and subsequent prejudice for anyone from Germany. Emil heard about opportunities in Philadelphia, and an area called Germantown where they could feel safe, surrounded by fellow German-speaking immigrants. The family moved shortly after Trudy's younger sister Frieda was born. Slowly, Emil was able to rebuild some of the wealth they had accumulated in Germany. Their oldest daughter, Trudy was a beautiful little girl with blonde ringlets, blue eyes and a bright smile that drew people in quickly. The family was surrounded by friends who shared a common history and language. They finally felt secure. They had no idea how quickly, and drastically, their lives were about to change. The Great Depression was on the horizon, and once again, Emil and Matilda found themselves struggling to survive. Emil's business collapsed, and they lost the money they had. With the little money they had stashed away literally under the mattresses, they decided the best thing for their young family was to get to a farm. They knew they could support themselves by living off the land. They made their way to an undeveloped, rural part of New Jersey. Trudy's earliest memories of life on the farm were complicated. It was idyllic with gardens and the animals, yet mixed with danger and excitement as her parents started having run-ns with the law.

The first time happened on a cold autumn night. Trudy and her two younger sisters were bundled up with plaid blankets and put into the family horse-drawn wagon. The girls were told to sit in a particular area in the wagon and instructed to keep still if they encountered other people along the way. Trudy's father guided the horses out of the barn and headed into town. Along the way, they were stopped by policemen on horseback carrying shotguns. They had a brief conversation with her father, and the officers began searching the wagon. She and her sisters never moved, as previously instructed by their mother. The family was eventually waved along their way, and the trip ended in an alley in the next big town over from the farm. The wagon was met by several men, who greeted Emil and Matilda warmly, yet quickly. At this point, Matilda turned to her daughters, and asked them to move from their warm spots. Her father fiddled with a latch under the blankets they had been sitting on, and to their surprise, there was a compartment stuffed with dark brown bottles filled with liquid. Transfers of bottles and cash happened quickly, and the next thing Trudy knew, she and her sisters were re-bundled and placed back into the wagon to head home. No explanation was given for what had just occurred.

Trudy would discover years later that her father was able to keep the farm and the family afloat by running alcohol during some of the Prohibition years. Sometime after the wagon incident, Trudy witnessed something much more sinister. Everyone was asleep, and Trudy was wakened by angry muffled voices below her bedroom window, near the back door. She crept out of her bedroom and watched in silence from the top of the stairs, as two very large men in long coats pushed her father against the door jamb. A third man emerged and Trudy could see a large scar on the man's left cheek. There were angry words, a flash of something that looked like a gun, and as quickly as they came, they disappeared into the dark night. She watched her father stagger back into the kitchen. He collapsed in his wooden chair at the head of the table. It was then that he heard a nose and caught sight of his oldest daughter crouched down at the top of the landing. "Gertrude" he whispered, "what are you doing up so late? Go back to bed."

There was no mention of this peculiar incident the next morning. Trudy's parents were very rigid and she knew there would be hell to pay if she were to ask him anything about what she saw. She told no one. Not even her sisters. The story would finally be told years later, Christmas Eve, 1964. After a few rounds of spiked eggnog, Trudy finally found her chance to ask her father about the night that left her with nightmares. To her utter amazement, she learned that the man at the door was Al Capone (Scarface), along with his two bodyguards who he never traveled without. Emil elaborated for his audience, who were sitting on the edge of their seats, mouths open. He said that as Capone's reputation grew, he insisted on being unarmed as a mark of his status. But he never went anywhere without at least two bodyguards when traveling by car. He preferred to travel under the cover of night, risking travel by day only when absolutely necessary. He would eventually become the czar of Chicago, running gambling, prostitution, and bootlegging rackets. The night Trudy saw him, Capone was upset about the bootlegging operation Emil was conducting and threatened Emil with serious repercussions if he didn't stop. For a few moments, the family was stunned into silence. Then everyone started recounting stories of the strange sights and sounds coming from the back of the barn, and the night they were the decoys sitting on top of the bootleg whiskey. Emil's illegal activity not only kept the family afloat, it would provide connections with a wealthy clientele that would save Trudy's life.

While out playing in the fields with the dogs, Trudy fell onto an old shovel hidden in the dirt. Raised to be very proud and independent, she cleaned herself up, and never mentioned it to her parents. A couple days later, she developed a fever, and her sister noticed a red stripe coming up from her ankle. By the time the story would come together so that Trudy's German-speaking parents understood what was happening, Trudy's legs were covered with boil-like sores. She became delirious, as her fever was raging. Desperate, her father reached out to one of his "secret" customers, a wealthy physician from Philadelphia. He examined Trudy, and said that with the speed the blood poisoning was occurring, he had to act quickly if they were going to save her legs. Dr. Schmidt knew he needed to let the poison out if she had any chance of ever walking again. He opened his black leather surgical bag, and took out several knives. He used alcohol and a flame from the lit stove burner to sterilize the instruments. Trudy was given some type of anesthetic to manage the pain, but methods were very crude in the early 1930's, in rural America. Dr. Schmidt made his incisions, and in some cases, cutting into the shin bones of each leg. Trudy's wounds were wrapped with bandages soaked in an herbal antiseptic solution that had been passed down through generations of women healers. Penicillin had been discovered in 1928, but wouldn't be commercially available until after World War II, around 1945. Dr. Schmidt additionally prescribed a diet consisting largely of bone marrow spread onto bread to support the buildup of new bone tissue. What they lacked in technology, they made up for with practical wisdom and ancient healing secrets.

Miraculously, over time, Trudy recovered with both her limbs intact. She would, however, have deep gouges along her shin bones of both legs. Trudy had gotten used to being teased for her thick German accent by the children in school. Now, as a young teenager, she decided it was best to cover her legs with thick stockings, even in the summer, to avoid new ridicule. It was around this time that the outgoing, happy child was replaced by an introverted self-conscious teenager. She put on weight as her body began changing during puberty; her obsession with her weight would plague her for most of her life. What Trudy had going for her were her survival instincts. She had proven herself a fighter, surviving the barbaric yet life-saving kitchen surgery a few years earlier.

Life for everyone changed dramatically as World War II wore on. As more men were drafted to serve, women were needed for jobs that only men had done previously. Trudy wanted to do her part, and she got the unlikely job as a large crane operator in the Philadelphia Navy Ship Yard. Trudy would joke about the stares she would get from the men in the shipyard as she climbed up into the crane … all five-foot-two of her, dressed in khaki overalls and a hard hat. She even overcame her fear of heights, to do her part for America. Years later, she would describe those few years as some of her favorites. She gained a sense of purpose beyond herself and an appreciation for her determination to go far out of her comfort zone. "It was a letdown after the war to go back to a desk," she would tell her younger sisters.

After the war she worked for a company in Center Philadelphia. It was during her lunch break when she literally ran into a young man at the Woolworth's lunch counter.

His name was Joe, and he worked around the corner at Globe Ticket Company as a machinist. They had an instant connection and became fast friends, meeting for lunch as often as they could. Joe lived in North Philadelphia with his Aunt and Uncle and Trudy lived with her parents over the bridge in South Jersey. Joe was thin, about five-foot-six with deep set brown eyes. Years later, many people would say he resembled the singer, James Taylor. His family also came through Ellis Island. After a short courtship, they were engaged. Joe surprised Trudy with a very special and significant ring. Like Trudy, he had experienced obstacles in his young life. His twin sister died during their birth, and he was what they called a "blue" baby. He had been born premature, not expected to live. He surprised everyone, only to have his mom die a few months later from childbirth complications. With the help of an older sister, his father did the best he could, but tragedy struck again. Joe's father died in an accident when Joe was just three years old, and he was raised by his aunt Josephine in a small apartment in North Philadelphia. Miraculously, Aunt Josephine had safely tucked away Joe's mother's engagement ring. Trudy understood deeply the significance of the ring as it was the only possession he had from his mother. There was a mutual understanding and appreciation for what they had both survived, and they looked forward with anticipation to the life they would create together.

Unfortunately, there would be more obstacles to overcome. Months before her wedding, Trudy was given the medical diagnosis that her uterus was full of fibroids. At that time, the prevailing treatment was a complete hysterectomy. She contemplated waiting to do the surgery until after her wedding, but her blood count was so low after years of losing blood that she was not given the option of waiting. So just months before her wedding day, she lost her ability to ever bear a child. Her two younger sisters would also receive similar diagnoses. All three sisters would never be able to start a family. Two years into Joe and Trudy's marriage, the desire to start a family intensified. Joe had been raised a devout Catholic, and they sought help from Catholic Charities to adopt an infant. However, Catholic Charities declined to help them. They were considered a mixed married couple as Trudy was Episcopalian, so they were turned away.

A work colleague recommended a lawyer who could help them. The terms included money upfront to cover fees and medical costs, and then the process of locating a baby would begin. Time was running out for them. They were on the edge of being ineligible to adopt, being in their mid-thirties; few questions were asked. Three months later, they received a healthy and beautiful baby girl, whom they named Elizabeth, after Joe's mother. She had light-brown hair, a button nose, and dark brown eyes. With loving adoptive parents and two sets of doting aunts and uncles, Elizabeth was cherished and showered with love and attention. Just shy of Elizabeth's first birthday, Trudy and Joe received a phone call from the lawyer. Initially thinking this was a normal follow-up call, they soon discovered the news was far from normal.

"Well, you see, sometimes, these things happen. You just can't predict. Women are so unpredictable, you know?" the lawyer stammered. "You'll need to return the baby. The birth mother has changed her mind."

Their beautiful Elizabeth had been secured by an unscrupulous lawyer, through a process referred to at the time as "the black market." Trudy and Joe quickly discovered they had no legal recourse and were informed that since the adoption wasn't done "legally," they had no options but to return their Elizabeth to her birth mother. Trudy sank into depression, barely able to get out of bed and dress for work. The thought of facing her friends and colleagues, and people in the local shops asking about Elizabeth, was more than she could bear. As time reduced the intensity of her pain, Trudy became more determined to adopt legally. They returned to Catholic Charities and explained that they would do whatever it took to adopt. Trudy would need to leave her faith, convert to Catholicism, and cover the adoption legal fees and medical costs in advance. They said "yes" immediately, having no idea how they could get that kind of money on Joe's machinist wages. A radical plan was agreed upon. They would sell their green Rambler, and Joe would walk to the train station, and travel across the bridge to downtown Philadelphia. Trudy would use the bus for errands. It was a sacrifice they were both willing to make. Miraculously, Trudy's younger sister, Frieda, and her husband Charles stepped in. They "loaned" Trudy and Joe the money for the adoption fees. There were many anxious hearts as Trudy and Joe, her sisters and their husbands, anxiously awaited the arrival of the new baby. This was Trudy and Joe's chance to start a happy new chapter in their lives together.

Sometime late August in 1956, Joe and Trudy's dreams were realized. They drove into center city Camden from their suburban home, and parked outside the large iron gate of the Catholic Diocese. It was foreboding to all who drove by. But not to Trudy and Joe on this day, as they were picking up their 10-week-old baby girl. They chose the name Christine, as she was the "light of their world." The initial excitement and joy Trudy felt, though, would be followed by other troubling emotions. Fear enveloped her as she worried that she could not maintain the standards Catholic Charities had imposed. Afterall, her first daughter had been taken away. Maybe she was not worthy of being a mother. Deep feelings of inadequacy would live in the shadows of Trudy's mind and impact those closest to her. I learned about my adoption when I was three years old.

Trudy and Joe had the perfect explanation. They told me, "Most parents have to keep what they get. In our case, we picked you because you're special." I grew up surrounded by my parents and two sets of aunts and uncles who loved me like the child they weren't able to have. It took years for my obvious questions to surface.

In the meantime, there were several anxious moments before I began school that let me know things were not entirely "normal" in our house. I sometimes heard strange sounds coming from the basement. It took me a while to get the courage to open the door to the cellarway to check it out. As I crept down the stairs, I saw my mother on her hands and knees frantically scrubbing the cement floor. I quietly backed up the stairs before she saw me knowing not to mention what I had seen. The next anxious moment directly involved me. My mother sewed beautiful dresses, decorated with lavish hand-stitched embroidery. Periodically she'd dress me up like a perfect little doll, and we'd travel on a train ride, ending at a large church-looking building. It had a formidable black ornate fence surrounding it and inside, wooden carvings and heavy drapes that made it hard to see anything. My mom was tense and worried. I recall a sense that it was important I "pass" inspection. Years later, I asked one of my aunts about the strange place. My mother and I had been in the main convent for the Sisters of the Catholic Diocese. She explained my mother's strange behavior in the basement and why we were at the convent. Trudy, she explained, was in constant fear the nuns would come to the house unannounced and inspect her housekeeping. Or they would see me during one of the convent visits, and would find something wrong. My mother's unarticulated "fear of losing me" was the driving force of her frantic behavior. Fortunately, none of my mother's fears of unannounced visits were realized and the trips to the convent finally ended. Her worries did not, and her resulting behaviors had an impact on me and my father. As I got older, I struggled to understand her manic/depressive behaviors, and the pressure I started to feel to be perfect in everything I did. My foundation was shaken to the core one night. While in my bedroom doing homework, I was interrupted by loud voices. I came out of my bedroom to check out what was happening. Two suitcases were sitting by the front door. I heard my mother say to my father, "I'm done. I've had enough. You figure it out." I remember the terror in the pit of my stomach, as I lunged at her legs, holding tight, begging her to stay.

She did stay… and her version of working it out meant not speaking directly to my father for weeks. No explanation was ever given as to what had precipitated such an event. My imagination ran wild. "Was it about me? I was doing the best I could. Did it have something to do with the 95% grade on my science test? She had been upset that it wasn't a perfect 100%. Dad had stepped in to defend me." I assumed the role of peace-maker between them and vowed to "do better." A truce was eventually established between them. For me, though, the damage was done. I had tried to understand the "why" behind her behaviors. Yet my predominant thoughts ranged from unworthiness to fear of abandonment; and were accompanied by two supporting characters, Sad and Mad. They would live in the shadows and rear their unpredictable behaviors as I entered my adolescence and later when I was a young adult. I survived by burying feelings I didn't feel safe expressing, deeper and deeper. It would take a life-threatening diagnosis to dive into the shadowy depths, years later.

Fortunately, my mom's younger sister Frieda offered me refuge during my teen years. Her given name morphed into Foots when I was a young child struggling with the correct pronunciation. An unbreakable bond was created with Aunt Footsie, that served as my lifeline. Well beyond her last breath at the age of eighty-six, our bond continues thirteen years later.

She was the one during the early years who had given me unconditional love and acceptance. No strings attached to my grade-point average, or performance on the hockey field. She also had an impact on my career choice. The guidance counselor at my college prep Catholic High School, steered me to a major where I could have a job AND raise a family. I recall sitting across from a woman who had given her life to God as a Dominican Sister, thinking "How can she give me advice about my life? I don't know if I even want kids." In 1970, there weren't many progressive counselors suggesting independent careers to young teenage girls. My aunt inspired me with her early work experiences after high school. At the time, she was dissuaded from applying for a job as a bank teller. The hiring manager said, "Women aren't capable of handling money because of their poor math skills." And as an additional insult, "You can't depend on them, because they get pregnant." Undaunted by the "belief of the day," my aunt became the first woman bank teller in Philadelphia. It became evident to everyone that she was smart, great with money, organized and efficient. She was featured in a newspaper article and became a catalyst for other women venturing into the male-dominated world of bank tellers. She took the road less traveled, and showed me what was possible with belief and focused determination.

3

PROMISES MADE

*"Acknowledging the good that is already in your life
is the foundation for all abundance."*

—Eckhart Tolle

There is a shared experience that most adopted adults can pinpoint. It's the exact moment when the reality of being adopted hits them. For some, it comes with incredible trauma as "someone slips" and they discover that their entire life has been a lie. Or for many Indigenous children who were taken from their parents, their tribes, and their culture, an inner knowing that they don't fit with their adopted families. For me, it happened during science class. Mr. Naughton began the morning with the science of genetics, and asked us to state our ancestry. Students began sharing where their grandparents and great-grandparents came from. When my turn came, I automatically responded, "German and Irish. My Mom's parents had come from Germany as the war escalated and my Dad's from Ireland, through Ellis Island." Moments later I was overcome with the realization that "I have no idea what my nationality was!"

How had I not seen this before? How could I miss this **not** so insignificant point? On my way home from school I thought, *the conversation at the dinner table is going to be very interesting tonight!*

Barely able to contain myself waiting for the right time to ask my question, I finally blurted out, "What is my **real** nationality?" I imagine they had dreaded the day this question would eventually surface. There was a long silence and shared glances between my parents. My mother was the first to speak. She said they just didn't know. Not the response I was expecting. She explained that the Catholic Charities adoption process was private and secret. The young birth mothers were told that their babies would have a better life with a couple that could care for them. The adopting parents were told horror stories of what could happen if the child were to discover their birth mother. Therefore, legal adoption documents were sealed away, and only a few pieces of non-identifying information were provided to the adopting parents. That night at the dinner table, I found out that my birth mother had lived somewhere in South Jersey, had gotten "into trouble," and was a teenager when I was born. They had no idea what her nationality was. The genetics class had awakened a sleeping bear, and I wanted more. I made a promise to myself that when I turned 18, I would find out my nationality and medical history. Fully understanding what my parents had experienced and sacrificed, no one, not even my aunt could know my plans. I knew that trying to explain that I needed more information would be translated as "they weren't enough". The risk of hurting them was too great, and not an option.

Not long after my adoption epiphany, my world turned completely upside down. It happened during my last few months of high school. I was excited to graduate and start college in the fall. Signs that there might be something wrong with my dad started to surface when he was in his mid-fifties. It happened after dinner occasionally at first. Then almost daily. He developed a condition where he had trouble keeping his food down. The doctor said that he had a nervous personality and they gave him medication to "calm his nerves." I watched as he gradually lost weight, and intuitively knew that his doctor was wrong. Around my mother's birthday in February, while lifting heavy equipment at work, Dad developed a hernia that needed to be surgically repaired. We lived just over the bridge from Philadelphia, and his doctor wanted him to go to University Hospital in the city for the procedure. The routine pre-operative blood work came back, and his hemoglobin (red blood cell count) was dangerously low. This meant that he was bleeding internally, somewhere. At that time, the only way to find out what was happening, was to do exploratory surgery. My mother and aunt waited in the Operating Room lounge, not anticipating the extent of the bad news they were about to receive. Hours later, the surgeon would tell them that dad had metastatic cancer. Which meant that when they opened him up, they saw the cancer had spread everywhere, and there was nothing more they could do. They closed the incision and took him back to his room. My aunt asked how long he had. "Well, we can never be certain," the surgeon explained. "It's a very aggressive and advanced cancer. He could die within the next two weeks. We'll do our best to keep him comfortable." My mother and aunt were waiting for me in the living room when I got home from school. It was obvious they both had been crying. "How did we get from 'Dad's just going in for a hernia operation,' to he'll be dead in two weeks?" I asked, trying to absorb the doctor's message. "His doctor missed this for over a year. He insisted dad's problem was due to his nervous constitution. He never did any tests. If he knew what he was doing, dad wouldn't be dying right now," I cried out.

Ten years later, I finally found solace. A surgical resident specializing in breast cancer was doing a rotation through our laboratory. She offered another perspective about the lack of an accurate diagnosis. Dr. Janet explained that the treatment at the time for patients with esophagus cancer consisted of a disfiguring surgery, followed by inserting a feeding tube to survive. She suggested he would have suffered for years, with no change in outcome. My father would never have wanted to be a burden to us. Her medical explanation helped me release the guilt I had carried all those years. My intuition had told me early on that something serious was wrong with him. There are no words that convey the agonizing pain of knowing you are going to lose your dad in two weeks, and there is nothing you can do to change it. What seemed especially cruel was I had just started to get to know him. I had exited the "know it all" phase of my early teen years, where I had no patience, and started to see him for who he truly was…a smart man of great patience and kindness. He had always accepted and supported my choices. And in many ways, nurtured me in ways my mother couldn't.

Dad died exactly 2 weeks after his diagnosis, totally alone in his hospital room. For my mom, the trip to the hospital in Northern Philadelphia was challenging both emotionally and logistically. Therefore, her visits were infrequent. The call from the hospital came on a Sunday evening, while mom and I were watching *The Wizard of Oz*. Not only did the flying monkeys and the melting wicked witch scare the heck out of me, I would forever associate anything Oz with my father's death. I sat silently as the reality that I would never see him again settled over me. There were no tears left to cry. I just felt numb. Later, as I struggled to fall asleep, a deep sadness enveloped me. I wasn't there to hold his hand, and tell him how much I loved him. The idea that someone should be alone in their final hours just tore at my heart. I vowed silently to my remaining family, "I promise to comfort and support you in your final moments as you cross over and take your last breath."

A few days after his funeral, I had the first of what can only be described as a "mystical" experience. Snow had started falling earlier in the day, and I looked forward to the possibility of no school the next morning. I awoke just past midnight to the sound of scraping noises as if snow was being shoveled. Why would anyone be out shoveling snow in the middle of the night, I wondered? I pulled back the heavy comforter, and crossed the dark room to my front window. My heart was pounding as I slowly pulled the curtain aside. I don't know what I thought I was going to see. Pressing my head against the cold glass, straining to get a better look in the darkness, the sound suddenly stopped. Fumbling my way back to bed, I wondered what had just happened. What tricks was my mind playing on me? Curiosity and apprehension about what I might discover in the morning kept me awake for a while. When I awoke, the sun was bright and shining through the curtains. As my feet hit the floor, the strangeness of the night before came to mind. Looking out the window, from a distance, it appeared our driveway had been shoveled. Pulling on my boots and parka to take a closer look, I rushed outside. The sidewalk had about six inches of undisturbed snow. The driveway, on the other hand, was clear down to the tar. Maybe a neighbor was trying to help us out, knowing Dad had died a few days earlier I reasoned? Except...

There were no footprints in the snow. Not one boot print! As I surveyed the situation, a soothing feeling came over me, and Dad instantly came to mind. That's when I remembered this had always been our thing together. I shoveled the porch steps and the sidewalk; Dad shoveled the much larger driveway. "What is this all about?" I wondered. "Is he letting me know he is somehow still here with me?" I ran back to the house and excitedly shared what had happened last night with my mother. And more importantly, my discovery in the light of day. Mom smiled and gave me a long hug. To her credit, she didn't discount my conclusion. She was still in shock over the unexpected passing of her husband, and especially worried about how she would manage the bills with him gone. I think she wanted to believe the same thing I did. That he was still around, and somehow, we would "be all right."

The second experience happened a few months later. It convinced me there was way more to life after death than I certainly understood. In what I can best describe as a waking dream state, I very clearly saw my father standing at the foot of my bed. He looked different from the last time I had seen him post-surgery, pale from the loss of blood, surrounded by monitors, and tubes poking out everywhere. 'This' Dad, standing at the foot of my bed, was smiling, vibrant and healthy. There was a luminosity around him, and I wasn't scared. He told me how much he loved me and that he was really proud of how I was looking after Mom. He explained he had stayed close since his leaving had happened so quickly, and had been "keeping an eye on us."

He continued that now it was time for him to go "further away." He emphasized he would still be watching us. This would be the last time I would experience him so directly and clearly. He asked me to trust what I felt when I thought of him. And to know that he was thinking of me at the same time. I woke up to a tear-stained pillow, and the recognition that something miraculous had happened. Dad's words offered a new understanding and comfort that he was only a thought away. I wondered if it was easier for our loved ones to communicate with us when we were in a dream state, when the doubting mind was off.

Wanting to know more about this experience, I asked my mom and aunts. They explained it away as "wishful" thinking. Except, I hadn't been thinking. What I did know for sure is my sadness lessened after that night, and for the first time since he died, I had hope of a path forward. I just didn't know what it was.

Dad's death the last few months of my senior year threw my college plans in total upheaval. I had been accepted into a small Catholic college in Horsham, Pennsylvania. Dad's company was relocating the summer before my freshman year in college and we had planned on moving. There was no money for me to go away to college, but with scholarships and commuting to Gwynedd Mercy College, my career plan was set. With Dad gone, and Mom struggling emotionally and financially, there was no way I could complete the plan of attending Gwynedd Mercy. My parents did not have mortgage insurance on the house, and after paying medical bills and the funeral, there wasn't much left from his life insurance policy. Narrowing my options further, my chosen major relied on a very specialized approach. The program offered a Bachelor's of Science in Medical Technology with a one-year internship at an approved teaching Medical Center. There were only 32 colleges in the country that offered this career and Gwynedd Mercy College was one of them. I had a passion for science and changing my major was not an option I wanted to consider. With all the changes, this would be one of the most challenging to maneuver through.

"What's the chance of finding another program close to home?" I worried aloud to my aunt.

Evidently high, as a branch of Rutgers University offered the same program at their South Jersey campus, in Camden.

This was great news as commuting was easy with the trains. I could keep an eye on my mother and accomplish my career goals. Rutgers gave me late acceptance and I started working as a phlebotomist at the Inner-city Hospital close to campus. Patient rounds started at 5:00 every morning and afterwards, I'd take the train to my classes. Between the early morning hospital rounds and the late nights on the train, I managed to survive the streets of Camden unscathed. I like to think my dad was operating as my "guardian angel."

Turning eighteen is a milestone birthday for most teenagers. My eighteenth birthday was noteworthy for reasons beyond the norm. This would be the first birthday without my dad, and the day I called Catholic Charities Adoption Agency to begin the quest for my birth mother's identity. Feeling my dad's blessing, I secretly made the call while my mother was out running errands. An additional catalyst for wanting to know my medical history had emerged. The relationship with my best friend in high school was progressing into something more serious. Dave was a year older, and while I was headed to college, he had moved to Chicago to apprentice as a glass blower. He was the youngest of four brothers, and unfortunately had experienced the deaths of multiple first cousins on his mother's side, from Cystic Fibrosis. If we were to marry in several years, not knowing if I potentially carried the gene would impact our decision about children. I had created a list of questions for my appointment with the social worker from Catholic Charities Adoption Agency. Going alone did not seem like a good idea, and with Dave in Chicago, I asked my best friend, Mike, to go with me for moral support.

Upon arrival, we were escorted to a small cubicle with a table separating us from the Social Worker, holding my files. She picked up a handwritten piece of paper from her desk, and was about to hand it to me, when I asked, "You have an official-looking folder that looks like it contains a lot of information. Am I going to receive that as well?" She responded, "You can't have the folder; however, I have this Xeroxed sheet from your folder." There were multiple black smears visible on what looked like an official record. She explained further, "The adoption records in the state of New Jersey are sealed. When the birth mothers agree to the adoption of their babies, no one has access to the information except Catholic Charities."

"My adoption was 18 years ago, surely things have changed since then?" I inquired. Incredibly, I would be asking this same question for the next three decades.

She handed me the sheet along with the handwritten note, adding, "Some states have opened their adoption records. New Jersey is not one of them." There was nothing of substance to read. The relevant information was underneath the black smudges. To know that I was so close to getting my mother's name and address, the hospital of birth, yet couldn't see through the black marks was beyond frustrating. I felt powerless and small. I set it down, as tears welled in my eyes. Hoping for more, I picked up the handwritten note. The note contained the following information:

My birth mother was seventeen when I was born.

Nationality was listed as Irish.

School records showed she was a good student and liked to dance.

Physical appearance included that she was five feet, five inches tall with a slight build, brown hair and brown eyes.

My voice began to break as I asked, "That's it?" The tears rolled down my cheeks and my emotions vacillated between sadness, frustration and downright anger.

"There's no mention of my birth father. What about him?" I asked.

"We aren't allowed to provide any information on fathers without the birth mother's consent," she responded.

"How long will it take?" I asked

"Since it's been 18 years, we have no way of contacting your birth mother."

"WHAT...." I exclaimed. "You don't keep updated information? Aren't the birth mothers required to report in, especially with any major health changes?"

This seemed like a very realistic question to ask, and the point where the meeting really went off the rails.

"We are not a detective agency. We do not follow the mothers nor do we require anything from them. What did you think you were going to receive today?" Her tone expressed frustration with my apparent lack of appreciation.

"I was looking for updated medical information. I am studying to be an Immunovirologist, and we now know many diseases are hereditary. I have a right to my medical history," I responded.

"I understand protecting the rights of the birth mothers, to a point. How about the rights of the adoptees?" I asked.

From the look on her face, I had clearly pushed her to her limit.

Her voice rose an octave. "Why is this so important? Do you have some type of disease?"

Taken aback and stunned at the insensitivity of her question, I managed to say, "I'm going to marry someone who has cystic fibrosis in his family. If there is cystic fibrosis in my ancestry as well, it's highly likely we would choose not to bring children into the world who might not live to see their thirteenth birthday."

She stood up, signaling our appointment was over. As she motioned us toward the door, she restated that they weren't a detective agency and I should be grateful for the information provided. Turning towards her as she closed the door, I was surprised by the absence of compassion on her face. Understanding she was bound by laws, there had to be a better way. Once we made it to the safety of the car, I doubled over sobbing. Mike offered compassionate support and we rehashed the few new facts revealed. My birth mother was Irish, we had the same hair and eye color, we were both good students, and both loved dancing. Discovery that we shared common traits left me wanting more. I resolved to never abandon my search efforts. This was just the beginning.

4

IT MATTERS TO THIS ONE

*"Our job is not to get out of our own way;
our job is to realize that we are our own way."*

—Matt Kahn

To enhance my chances of getting into college, my mother had insisted I take up a musical instrument. I agreed to join the concert band only. I was not going to give up field hockey for marching band. It was there that I met Dave. He played the sousaphone, and was a grade ahead of me. He was the only person I knew in high school who voluntarily read Rollo May, Carl Jung, and Aristotle. We became friends, and after fifty years of knowing each other, it brings me great joy that he's my husband and still my best friend. Interestingly, Dave is much like my father, kind, supportive, and compassionate. We discovered early in our friendship that we shared many of the same dreams, desires, and questions about life. The most significant centered around our Catholic upbringing and our desire to find the "real truth." Dave had similar experiences in grade school with the inconsistencies and hypocrisies taught in the classroom. They didn't seem to match Jesus' teachings from the gospels in the New Testament. We compared notes about the moment we knew something was drastically wrong. The first moment I took on authority and stood up for the rights of others happened when I was ten. In front of the classroom, the priest made a startling statement: "Only Catholics go to heaven. We are the true Church."

Somehow, my hand shot up in the air. "How could the children in China be sent to hell?" I asked. "They didn't have a choice where they were born, or what culture they grew up in. What you're saying makes no sense." His response was even more infuriating. "That's why missionaries are so important. They educate and change people's beliefs so they can come around to the right way of thinking." Not satisfied with his answer, I continued, "This does not align with Jesus' teachings." Needless to say, a phone call was made to my parents. Though they chastised me, I always felt they also were proud of me.

Several months later, during a special children's mass, the monsignor told us we couldn't play with the Protestant kids or even talk to the Jewish kids because they were "Inferior religions." This was the last straw. I informed my parents that I was no longer going to church. Truly a challenging position for my mother after her conversion to Catholicism where she had to promise to raise her child Catholic. Not to be denied, I pleaded my case to my dad. A compromise was arranged; when I entered junior high, I could stop going to church weekly. It was a done deal that I would attend the college prep Catholic High School. I made a commitment that the truth was out there, and I would find it.

Fortunately, Dave shared the same vision, and we agreed that someday, we would "find the truth." Not only did I find a kindred spirit, I inherited a second mom. Dave's mother Marie, like my dad, also defied the odds and survived a premature birth. She raised four boys, while working several nights and weekends to supplement the family's income. Marie had been the oldest sister to six brothers growing up during the Depression. When Dave introduced us, she welcomed me like the sister and daughter she never had. My mother had become more fragile and emotionally unstable after my father's unexpected death. Marie came into my life when I needed a compassionate listener and a confidante when the pressures of caring for my mom overwhelmed me. Marie also became a safe haven each time I encountered rejections and failed attempts to find my birth mother. My appreciation is deep for her unconditional love, sisterhood, and hilarious family stories. The world was fortunate to have her for ninety-eight wonderful years.

Dave and I married two days after my college graduation and a week before my twenty-second birthday. Our families seemed to recognize we were destined for each other, as no one pushed back that we were too young for marriage. Dave's closest brother, Bill, did predict that we would only last six months. I like to tease him that we've stayed together this long, just to prove him wrong. With no extra money to spare, our wedding was a simple affair. We had a candlelight Friday night service, followed by a reception at my mother's house. Shortly before my dad died, he had put on a "rec room" addition, which would be able to hold fifty family members and friends. My mom made my dress AND the wedding cake. The happiness of the occasion was overshadowed by the fact that as soon as the reception ended, Dave and I got into my four-door, three-speed on the column Plymouth Belvedere and drove to Chicago. I had secured a laboratory position in a hospital in Chicago, and moved right into Dave's apartment.

Even with the reassurances from my aunts that they would look after my mother, I left the house with significant anxiety and guilt. This was made worse when my mother told me before the wedding, "Just leave. No good-byes." While understandable, it was still heart-wrenching. My father was not there to walk me down the aisle or comfort my mother as her only daughter was getting married and moving sixteen hours away. The first three years of marriage would prove the most challenging. I had moved from my mother's house to my husband's apartment, never experiencing living alone. The realization that I had no idea "who I was" outside my family's values and beliefs was unsettling at best. At the same time, I trusted that somehow, we would figure it out.

Our first apartment together was a one-bedroom unit on the third floor of an old brick building in Rogers Park (north Chicago). Newly married, with college loans to repay, and just starting our careers, we looked for ways to save money. Always industrious, Dave collected the trash for the units in our building and in the cold Chicago winters, shoveled snow. And in return, we received a discount on our rent. We were young, with limited resources, and excited to find the "meaning of life."

We began with the local Presbyterian Church that Dave's older brother Bill recommended. Also a scientific glassblower, Bill had moved to Chicago a couple of years earlier, and was the reason Dave was learning the same craft. The sermons were messages of inclusion, and we were intrigued with the church's social activism. On a very cold Chicago night in early 1979, about eight months after the wedding, the church sponsored a talk given by a young couple who had recently returned from Guatemala. Their focus was building houses with the local villagers and providing ownership and independence for the families.

They also talked about an opportunity much closer to home. They described a small area on the border of North Chicago and affluent Evanston. It was just a few blocks from Lake Michigan, and at one time it had been a very affluent white neighborhood. Mostly brick, three-flat apartment buildings with interesting architectural designs made up the several blocks of this lakeside neighborhood. Unfortunately, sometime in the mid 1950's, the city constructed a turn-around for the new train station on the east side of the neighborhood. The assembly of tracks generated intense screeching noises from the elevated trains coming in and out of the city. The affluent moved out, and buildings emptied. Properties were bought up by absentee landlords, and over time drug dealers began to outnumber the working families. The couple speaking at the church program, Nancy and Joe, described the many challenges the neighborhood currently faced.

A staggering example was there were more than thirty languages spoken in the first-grade class! Nancy and Joe articulated a vision about what was possible with resources and volunteers. The neighborhood had recently been adopted by a house church in Evanston affiliated with Northwestern University. It was overseen by two Presbyterian ministers who had met and marched with Martin Luther King. Undergraduate and graduate students, like Joe and Nancy, offered their talents in partnership with neighborhood leaders to provide solutions. The most pressing needs dictated the priority projects, which included an alternative grade school, after-school reading program, teen drop-in center, an emergency shelter for women and children, and the most daunting … the renovation of a transient hotel. The hotel would get people off the streets, while they received the help they needed to get back on their feet. It was the first time I heard the phrase "Doing God's work in the world." Dave and I looked at each other, knowing that this group was the answer to our prayers as we searched for our life's purpose. Would we find God in this abandoned neighborhood now called Good News North of Howard? Moved by Nancy and Joe's vision and hope, we donated my old Plymouth Belvedere that we were planning to sell later that month. Someone spotted her years later in Guatemala, delivering food and medicine out into the villages.

We attended the Sunday night inter-faith community services at the house church on the Evanston campus. I was blown away! It was a place where people of all faiths came together, committed to making the world a better place. We decided to move from the safer part of Rogers Park into a three-room apartment, with roommates, in the middle of Good News North of Howard. Since I had commuted to college and grew up an only child, having roommates for the first time -- and a new husband -- proved tricky at best. To say it was eye-opening would not quite do the experiences justice! My time in the neighborhood proved to be *the* most challenging of my adult life. My limiting beliefs were constantly challenged as Dave and I decided to volunteer as the leads for the weekend drop-in center for the young teens. It had been started by Frank, a giant of a man with a heart that equaled his size. Every Friday and Saturday night, we ventured down our back ally to the drop-in center on Paulina Street to staff the center. The kids were smart and funny; they had been dealt a hand I could never envision coming from a suburb in New Jersey. Most, if not all of the children, came from households with no dad present. Their moms worked two or three jobs to provide the basic human needs: food and shelter. It was all about survival for the mothers and their children. My big wakeup call came one day when I was talking to a particularly studious fellow named Anthony. His friends lovingly called him the "Professor," because he wore big old-style black-rimmed glasses, and was a straight-A student. I casually asked him one night during a game of foosball where he was going to college. He was a junior at the time and should already be selecting schools. He looked at me like I was crazy.

He said, "College? How am I possibly going to go to college? I don't know if we're going to be able to stay in our apartment next month." I asked him, "What about scholarships? Isn't your guidance counselor talking with you and helping you apply for funding?" The answer was no. And that's when I realized what privilege really meant and how much I had taken for granted.

He invited me to his home to meet his mom. The three of them lived in a tiny one-bedroom apartment. His mom was fixing dinner for Anthony and his sister, and then she was heading back out to her second job as a nurse's aide. Anthony's "bedroom" was a bed pushed against the windows in the kitchen with a curtain separating his space from the rest of the kitchen. His desk was the shelf of the window sill. His sister slept with his mom. I had the opportunity to share with Anthony's mother what a leader he was in the drop-in center, and asked her if anyone from his school had mentioned college applications and scholarship? Tears welled in her eyes as I talked about her son. Lines of exhaustion and sadness were etched on her face. She was doing everything she could to keep her children safe and cared for. She didn't have any experience with what it would take to help her son be eligible for college. She was functioning in pure survival mode.

Anthony graduated from high-school with honors and was accepted at a downtown college on a scholarship. It was a real win for him, his family, and his friends, serving as inspiration for them, too. Unfortunately, these outcomes seemed few and far between. The more time and support we were able to offer, there always seemed so much more that needed to be done. Most pressing was an afterschool tutoring program. A chance to give the children a safe place off the streets, while their moms were working.

A particularly hard reality to face was that even when I thought we were doing everything possible to stop the cycle of a one-parent family, and teen pregnancies, they continued to happen. One particular situation really illuminated for me the generational impact on these children. There was a very popular and well-liked high school couple that came to the center most weekend nights. It provided them a safe place to hang out and be with their friends. We talked openly about preventing pregnancy and even hosted Planned Parenthood talks for the kids that wanted to come. Our favorite couple, Tanya and Robert, shared news of Tanya's pregnancy one Saturday night as the Drop-In center was closing. They told us not to worry, and mapped out the plan that mirrored how they had both been raised. Tanya's mother already worked two jobs; however, her grandma was willing to help raise the baby so Tanya could continue with school. My heart sank, imagining how much harder her already difficult life was going to become.

True to her word, Tanya did graduate high school. Relieved that she had, I still felt like we had failed them. There was no shortage of need in this forgotten neighborhood, now being used as a drug supply warehouse for the wealthy driving down from the North Shore. I felt as if we were plugging one hole in the dam, only to have three more spring open. I began to experience the symptoms of burn-out. I had put myself into the role of guardian and protector for these children, a surrogate mother. Yet, I wasn't able to give them everything they needed to feel safe and succeed in the world. People at work would ask when I was going to become a mother. I just smiled, realizing there were a whole bunch of teenagers out there who already had my heart. And after seven years of running the center every weekend, it was time to head back to New Jersey. My own mother needed me, as her health was failing.

Feeling like a failure as I prepared to leave for New Jersey, inspiration came from an unlikely source. It happened to me while shopping for a birthday card. Do you know the Starfish Story? To paraphrase … there's a person walking on the beach, and as she looks up ahead, she sees someone reaching down for something on the sand, and then tossing it into the ocean. Moving closer, the woman sees that the beach at the water's edge is covered with starfish. It was then she realized it was a man picking up one starfish at a time with great intention, and placing them back into the water. "What are you doing?" the woman asked. "There are so many, what does it matter? You can't save all of them." The man picked up a beautiful 5-pointed red starfish. Looking at it closely he said, "It matters to this one," gently placing it back into the water for the waves to carry it safely from the beach. With tears in my eyes, I realized this was the answer to my sense of failure for not "doing enough" in Chicago. I couldn't help all the children we met at the drop-in center. And I couldn't reverse decades of trauma. I could give my love and intention to each one of the children in the drop-in center. I was able to let them know they were *seen* and that they *mattered*.

We found it was impossible to be socially active without also becoming politically aware. I found myself becoming involved on a much bigger scale than the Earth Day rallies I led in high school. The most humbling and belief-altering experience happened right before leaving Chicago.

The house church community was committed to helping end the arms race that had built up during the Reagan administration. Federal money was being diverted from essential food and services program to fund the arms race. During the lead-up to one particularly important Congressional vote, a rally cry was sent out for people to come together and make a united statement for peace at the Pentagon. A group of us from Northwestern and Good News North of Howard came together with our "Bread Not Bombs" T-shirts and posters, and left Chicago for the long bus ride to Washington DC. It was the most exhilarating road trip ever! We joined together with thousands of other like-minded folks, and encircled the Pentagon. Late in the day, I had to use the bathroom. I decided to venture inside the Pentagon. Proudly wearing my T-shirt, I walked up the steps, through the entrance doors to use the public restroom in the lobby. I passed a woman coming out of the Pentagon who worked inside. She looked at my T-shirt, and paused. She said with conviction, "You know, I believe that what I'm doing here is bringing about world peace!" And then she continued on her way. I stood frozen on the steps. For the first time in my life, I experienced the duality of a situation with great clarity. There were two beliefs, equally true for each of us. We were just looking from different perspectives. It had honestly not occurred to me until then that there were good people with sincere feelings of conviction on the other side of this issue. I rejoined Dave in the circle, and shared my encounter. We talked about the implications during the bus ride back to Chicago. One of the many insights from the experience was the realization that the world is not black and white. There are many shades of grey.

I could see that if we had any chance for a lasting solution there had to be communication to find the common vision. Demonizing and making others wrong for having a different perspective just creates more divisiveness and entrenchment into long-held beliefs. And what are beliefs, anyway? They are just thoughts we continue to think. And our thoughts can be changed. Which can happen through meaningful dialogue and a pure intention to find solutions. I remain eternally grateful for that woman on the steps who ignited a spark that continues to burn as I endeavor to find the common thread with those around me, in all areas of my life. You never know where the transformational moment is going to happen. It could be in a Hallmark store at the mall, or on the steps of the Pentagon. Or from a hippie roommate.

Chicago had delivered new ideas around social and political activism, and incredible insights into my limited beliefs. Our last roommate in Chicago impacted our spiritual understanding before we left for New Jersey. He introduced us to his favorite books and authors: Thoreau, the Tao, Gandhi, Black Elk, and Yogananda. An unraveling of spiritual beliefs had begun and it became obvious to both Dave and me that even the label "Christian" was restrictive. I thought it was a big leap to go from calling ourselves Catholic to attending an "inter-denominational Christian house church." Now it felt like jumping off a cliff, recognizing the big difference between spirituality and religion. It seemed to me that there were many beliefs and religions, and like rivers, they were all running toward the same ocean. In second-grade religion class, I seemed to intuitively know this as I challenged the priest's declaration about children in China doomed to hell because they weren't born Catholic.

Not knowing how to put these understandings into practice yet, we concluded there was a marked difference between spirituality and religion. I found myself very drawn to the Indigenous Shamanic view of the interconnectedness and the sacredness of the earth, and all her inhabitants. We had arrived in Chicago seven years earlier with a prayer to 'find meaning and purpose and to know God.' It appeared that we had been set onto a new path with additional questions to explore.

Most pressing for me was, "Who am I and why am I here? Am I a spiritual being having a human experience? Or a human being having spiritual experiences?"

These questions would ultimately lead to an unexpected spiritual journey that included Eastern philosophies. I was definitely branching out from the inter-faith house church at Northwestern.

5

JOURNEY TO RECOVERY

"You are afraid of surrender because you don't want to lose control. But you never had control, all you had was anxiety."

—Elizabeth Gilbert

Taking care of my mom back in New Jersey became an important next step in my spiritual journey. As I worked on integrating so many of the life-altering experiences I had in Chicago, unresolved issues that I had buried or ignored began to bubble up. It began as I was completing a Graduate Teaching program I had begun in Chicago, while also starting a new immunovirology position in Philadelphia. My secret had started to manifest in Chicago. The combination of starting a new career, volunteering, living with roommates, and being newly married proved to be too much for my coping strategies. I didn't know it had a name and label till I saw it on a poster in the women's bathroom at Pennsylvania Hospital. The poster asked a few questions that stopped me in my tracks:

Do you exercise to an extreme?
Do you sometimes binge on large amounts of food?
Do you identify as being fat, but people disagree?
Do you eat in secret?
Have you lost your period?

The small print referenced these symptoms as signs that you might have an eating disorder. I was confronted with the cold reality that what had been working as a coping mechanism had set me on an unhealthy and dangerous path. And it had a name: exercise bulimia. Not realizing it at the time, the desire to research and learn more was a very positive step forward. It meant for the first time, I was strong enough and *willing* to explore the truth about my secret behaviors.

Some of the seeds had been planted when I was a young child. My mother had labeled me as "chubby", which was the reason I quit ballet after eight years. Feeling fat compared to the other girls became so painful that I decided facing my mother's disappointment and "being called a quitter" was a better alternative than going back to the ballet studio. What saddens me now is that looking back at old family photos, I see an athletic young girl, not a chubby one. My mother was obsessed with her weight, and her unconscious projection onto me set the stage for my unhealthy body image. It would have a hold on me from about the age of eleven, all the way to my mid-thirties. After my dad died during my senior year of high school, February 1974, I started to gain weight. Getting married and leaving my mother as I moved to Chicago, along with starting a new job which required passing the American Society for Clinical Pathology Registry exam, set up the perfect storm for even more weight gain. Life was moving fast, and there were many things beyond my control. Using food to avoid uncomfortable feelings became a hardwired pattern and coping mechanism to which I was blind. Many years later, the term "psychological blind spot" helped explain how my behavior had been enabled for so long. As it was happening, I just didn't see it.

It was at this point, in my mid-twenties, where my weight crossed the line from athletic to not healthy. A work colleague started an aggressive exercise and weight-loss program, and I was inspired to follow in her footsteps. I started my program in November and went through all the holiday parties, starving myself and exercising. I lost thirty pounds in just eight weeks. Initially, I looked and felt amazing. Eventually, an acute fear of losing control and gaining it back consumed and overwhelmed me. To avoid this possibility, I increased my exercise program. At its peak it included:

- Riding my bike to work every day.
- If it was snowing, walking the five miles to and from work. After all, I couldn't risk not burning calories that day!
- Two aerobic classes/day on campus when possible.
- Swimming a mile at least two or three times a week.

And I managed to do this while surviving on rice cakes, low-calorie cheese, raw broccoli, and salads. Until out of the blue, something would trigger me and I "had" to have my favorite binge foods. Looking back, they were my comfort foods linked to a simpler time, when I was a child.

Binging triggered a cycle of more exercise or calorie restrictions to compensate for the excess calories. At my darkest point, my survival was linked to denying there was anything unusual about my addictive behaviors. Doesn't everyone bike to work, swim multiple miles a week and take daily aerobics classes, while consuming raw veggies and rice cakes? Acknowledging or talking about my excessive behavior with someone one would only trigger their desire to make me stop. And how could I stop? I became acquainted with the never-ending cycle of an addiction that totally consumed me. What's so perverse about addiction is the inability to even enjoy whatever the blocking behavior of choice happens to be. For me, my binge foods of choice brought me minutes of relief, followed by hours of remorse. I didn't even get to enjoy being "thinner." At a size five, my distorted body image and inner voice still labeled me as fat. As a functioning addict, no one knew the amount of food I ate, or how much exercise I did in a day. It would become an all-consuming process I managed hourly. Who would have guessed an accomplished immunovirologist, enrolled in a prestigious graduate program at Northwestern while volunteering with "Good News North of Howard," was dying on the inside?

By the time I left Chicago at the age of thirty, there was so little body fat on my frame that hormonal imbalances caused amenorrhea, a condition where I no longer had a monthly cycle. Knowing how potentially damaging this was, I chose to stay in denial. Living back home with my mom after eight years of independence was more challenging than I anticipated. I had no place to retreat or the ability to control my environment. Our challenging relationship was still challenging, and triggers for my coping behaviors were abundant. My destructive patterns were increasing by the day. An intervention was necessary, yet who could intervene when to the outside world I appeared completely in control? Miraculously, the words I memorized from the poster I saw in the women's bathroom while working that day at Pennsylvania Hospital reached a part of me that was ready to seek help. Seeing my behaviors on a poster associated with a medical diagnosis jolted me awake to how far from reality I had slipped. It happened just in the nick of time!

The first step in my recovery was admitting I needed help. Dave had noticed my mood swings and erratic behaviors, and thought they were a result of the move back home, a new job, and finishing my graduate studies. He was shocked to discover the truth, and willing to do whatever I needed to become healthy. I found a doctor who specialized in hormonal imbalances, and she immediately put me on hormones to get my body working properly again. I braced myself for the obvious side effect … weight gain! I would continually confront the choice to get back in balance and gain weight, or stay "thin," and slowly destroy my body.

I had not found Integrative Healing Philosophies yet, which considered all aspects of body, mind and spirit as critical for sustained long-term healing. The doctor's treatment for amenorrhea focused on my physical body to trigger a normal monthly cycle, yet ignored the emotional distress the weight gain created. I retreated into a cocoon of protection I wove for myself, and pushed people away. The emotions rising to the surface as I tried to stop the endless cycle of overeating and exercising became overwhelming. My marriage was tested during this journey into recovery. Mercifully, there were times when I was in nature or playing with the cat, that a distant voice inside found its way to the surface.

The message was clear…keep moving forward, one step at a time, and follow your path. The Taoist quote, "A journey of a thousand miles begins with a single step", became a touchstone and symbol of hope and determination. The message became quite literal while walking to the train on a very cold January morning. A potential path took the form of a flier on a lamp post. It was an invitation to an Overeater's Anonymous Meeting. I went that evening after work, having no idea what would happen. The success stories of people overcoming addiction and having a lifetime of sobriety thanks to Alcoholic Anonymous are extraordinary. I was curious how Overeaters Anonymous (OA) could work. A person has to eat!

Sitting on the cold metal chair, looking at the faces in the circle, it was evident that this "eating thing" did not discriminate by sex, age, color, or religion. The group leader started the meeting and people shared how they were powerless over food. There were stories similar to mine, which offered a confirmation that I was in the right place. As the sharing continued, something caught my attention. People were describing their "problem/condition" as something they would deal with their entire lives. The solution was recognizing our powerlessness over food, and turning the daily struggles over to a higher power. Memories from my Catholic School religion classes were triggered. I had always questioned the distinction between grace and self-effort. And I never understood the Church's role as an intermediary outside of myself that would do the saving and forgiving on my behalf. For me, it was un-empowering and reinforced feelings of unworthiness. On my walk home, there was significant inner dialogue:

This isn't drugs or alcohol. It's food. Something I have to interact with every day. There has to be a reason why this is happening. I don't want to just treat the symptom and not find the root cause of the dis-ease. What if my behavior is a symptom of an underlying problem and once I understand it, I can heal and move beyond it? Is there an even bigger message?

It would be years before I fully appreciated the power of what happened that night. I had crossed a threshold into contemplation, empowerment and possibility, after being brought to my knees. It appeared I was slowly moving beyond the mind's view of the situation. While the ego asks, "How can I make this different?" The soul asks, "How is this beneficial for my soul's evolution?" The OA meeting was a gift and the catalyst that propelled me towards real recovery. One thing was certain: I needed to find a more holistic path. In that moment, I had no idea what it was or where it might lead.

Months later, Dave had an opportunity to start a new and exciting glassblowing position in a company outside of Boston. New England was a place where we had vacationed numerous times, and it was on the short list of places to live once my mother stabilized. We discussed as a family the possibility that she could move in with us if her condition deteriorated. I left home for the second time, reassured by my aunts and mom's friends that they would take good care of her. We found a small, blue ranch-style house with white shutters and a picket fence, just over the border in New Hampshire. Eight years of being married so far and we finally had our own home. No more coordinating and negotiating with roommates or parents. Only one adopted black and white kitty from our time in Chicago to demand our attention. The house was surprisingly affordable. The realtor explained that the value was depressed because it was "across from the projects," and hard to sell.

Dave and I laughed out loud. "Seriously? Clearly the people in this Nashua neighborhood have not lived in the inner-city of Chicago surrounded by real projects," we explained to the realtor. Across from our house was a small row of apartments for low-income families, and on the next block over, a Girls and Boys club. The neighborhood was clean and well-cared for, and to the best of anyone's knowledge, no one had been stabbed on the sidewalk, or had a gun fight in the middle of the day, as we had experienced in Chicago. The natural beauty of New England with its deep glacier lakes, boulder-filled rivers, mountains with hiking trails and the healing sound of the Atlantic Ocean is food for the soul. I believe we were guided to this beautiful, nurturing place, where I could heal and explore new possibilities.

Our privacy would last about a year. Mom had the first of many minor strokes, called TIAs. Fortunately, with this first one, she suffered no permanent paralysis. Fearing it would be more serious next time and she would be home alone; we all agreed the best way for her to be safe was to have her move in with us. Being realists, Dave and I recognized we would need a larger house, preferably with an in-law apartment. We found a great house with lots of potential, and closed a few days before Christmas. Not to miss my mother's favorite holiday, we strategically packed the U-Haul truck with kitchen items and her favorite Christmas decorations at the back of the truck. Snow began to fall as we unloaded the truck while my mother decorated the Christmas Tree we had picked up on the way to our new home. Everyone was exhausted and thankful. There was peace that Christmas in knowing the right decision had been made. She would be safe with us.

Dave started his new job, and I left New Jersey with my new graduate degree in Education, and a dream to find a position where I could combine my love of teaching with my immunovirology lab experience. Putting out inquiries to Medical Industry Leaders I had met while working in Chicago, I discovered there were multiple sales openings in the New England area. Being a technical person, I had envisioned a technical specialist position where I could teach people how to run the new equipment in the laboratories, as well as troubleshoot. Incredibly, a few months after my inquiries, I received a phone call that the very position I had described had been created at Abbott Laboratories. They were starting a new specialty team which included twenty-four Medical Technologists to accelerate the implementation of screening the nation's blood supply for the HIV virus. AIDS – stands for Acquired Immune Deficiency Syndrome disorder – had become a serious health-care challenge with more and more people contracting the disease through donated blood products. At that time, the prognosis included a slow and debilitating demise with almost certain death.

The day after I found out about the opportunity with Abbott, a second opportunity presented itself. A choice would need to be made. On one hand, Abbott was a trail-blazing role, never done before. The second option was safe and familiar. I wish I could say it was a "no-brainer." After all, the first position with Abbott was literally what I had described to them months earlier! Dave came through with the right question at the right time accompanied by an effective challenge disguised as a safety net:

"What's the worst that can happen? If it doesn't work out, you can always go back to the lab and the comfortable choice."

I faced my fears and took the road less traveled. My aunt would have been pleased.

6

HEALING THE HUNGRY HEART

*"Lift the veil that obscures the heart, and there
you will find what you are looking for."*

—**Kabir**

The choice to take the road less traveled was enlightening in many ways. One was quite literal, as I travelled all over New England, teaching the technologists in hospital laboratories. The job itself was extremely fulfilling, as getting the major blood centers up and running as soon as possible was a matter of life-and-death for blood recipients. I thrived in the flexibility of not working a nine-to-five job. The problem solving, collaborating with colleagues and helping customers and their patients proved very satisfying. There were many successes and I thrived. But an unanticipated contention emerged between my mother and me. As I brought awards home after our large company meetings, my mother would innocently comment,

"Congratulations, Chrissy. I knew you could do it. You're just like me." Or my other favorite, "You are your mother's daughter." These comments had the opposite effect, with my prevailing thought being, "I'm nothing like you." Resentment slowly surfaced and it became an all-too-familiar companion. I stopped sharing my accomplishments with my mother as our relationship deteriorated. Tensions increased in the house, and Dave's natural disposition of calm understanding and tolerance was pushed to its limits. He did not ask, he demanded, that I get help!

I had made progress with my eating disorder with the help of a nutritional therapist. However, with my mother and I together again, emotions were triggered, and buried feelings began to surface. Fortunately, a solution wasn't too far away. A few months earlier, I was introduced to a very talented massage therapist who became our next spiritual resource guide and great friend. Kathy introduced us to the writings and recordings of Deepak Chopra and Wayne Dyer. Studying quantum physics and ways to live in the present moment proved to be exactly the right next steps for our spiritual journey that had begun in Chicago. She also recommended a psychologist friend who used NLP (Neuro Linguistic Programing) as part of his healing and counseling modality. I booked an appointment and eagerly awaited the chance to explain to an expert my "mother's" problem. The first meeting began predictably. He asked for an overview of the problem and listened without interruption as I described my mother as a fragile, yet manipulative woman in her early 70s. I explained that no matter how much we did for her, it was never enough. We did all her favorite things, like taking scenic drives and going to her favorite restaurants, only to discover while talking to my aunts, that the picture my mother painted was quite different. She told her sisters that she rarely saw us. John, a Neuro-Linguistic Programing

(NLP) practitioner and therapist, asked me how I felt about this experience. I expressed my frustration for her lack of appreciation and playing the role of victim. I shared that progress had been made with a therapist, until the recent new job and living situations arose. John explained that he would like to use NLP as a process to safely connect to my buried feelings, so they could finally be released. Interestingly, beneath the anger and resentment, feelings of "not being good enough" were hiding out. John suggested an interesting next step. He and Kathy, who my mom knew and loved, would come to dinner to give him a chance to observe the family dynamics. It was an intriguing and unique approach, for sure.

Anxious to hear his assessment during our second appointment, I could barely restrain myself. "Did you see what I described?" He smiled, and offered a different perspective. "I saw a capable woman, in control. I did not experience her as weak or helpless. I did observe that she adores you."

Seriously? I was shocked. *How could he not see what I was up against?*

Living together had created an environment of resentment and misunderstanding. His next words were profound and became the catalyst that would eventually heal my broken relationship with my mother.

John emphatically stated, "You are not responsible for her happiness. You are not responsible for anyone's happiness except your own. Happiness is not dependent on the behavior of others."

His words resonated inside as a core truth, a knowing, long forgotten. Sitting in silence, tears began to stream down my face. The pieces began coming together. My belief that I was responsible for her happiness had robbed both of us of contentment, replacing it with the destructive pain of resentment. Years of counseling that started in New Jersey for my eating disorder had not been as powerful as three sessions with John. He recommended a recently published book called *Feeding the Hungry Heart,* by Geneen Roth. She recounts her time as an emotional eater and self-starver and how, after years of struggle, she finally broke through the destructive cycles. I purchased the small paperback and could not read it fast enough. Every word, every sentence, rang true for me. By the time I finished the book, there were turned down page corners and yellow highlights everywhere.

I wondered how I had **not** recognized the eating disorder behaviors as effective blocking mechanisms, keeping my feelings and emotions buried? It seemed anger, sadness, and unworthiness were the ones I wanted the most distance from. Geneen Roth's honest sharing of her battle and subsequent recovery process set me on a new path of wholeness and recovery. She helped me see the battle was against a hunger that went way deeper than my need for comfort food. It would take more time and deep and honest introspection to fully understand and embody that true acceptance can only come from within.

Identifying and sitting with emotions I had spent years avoiding turned out to be a game changer. This quote offered wonderful encouragement:

> "Courage is not the absence of fear ... but the recognition that there is something stronger and more powerful inside than the fear itself."

With the support of Geneen's book, and mindfulness practices like yoga and meditation, the eating disorder faded from my reality. It was no longer needed. I recalled the determined voice when leaving the Overeater Anonymous meeting years earlier, "What you are experiencing is a symptom. Find the root cause, and the behavior will go away."

While deep into my self-healing work, Dave continued to explore spiritual philosophies and paths of enlightenment. Eastern philosophies continued to resonate and align with the oneness beliefs from Indigenous cultures. There was a particular event that opened up the next pathway to explore. It occurred innocently enough, while we were having dinner with Kathy and her new friends. George had been to India and lived at Yogananda's Ashram in California for a while. He suggested a reading list that included *Play of Consciousness* by Swami Muktananda, and mentioned off-handedly that there was an Ashram in the Northeast, with a living meditation master and spiritual teacher. As an introduction, George loaned us a video of Gurumayi Chidvilasananda chanting sacred mantras at her Ashram in Ganeshpuri, India. George strongly suggested we be in an open and receptive state. The chant was in a language unknown to us, yet I felt a profound pull inward and a feeling of deep peace. There was also a tingling at the crown of my head, which created a sensation of expansion. When the video concluded, Dave and I sat in silence. The experience was beyond words. We had to know more. An unexpected event in an unlikely place provided the answer we were looking for.

We had planned a trip with Kathy and her new friends to Philadelphia for a workshop on a Spiritual Philosophy from Hawaii, called Ho'oponopono. *With its focus on "forgiveness," it seemed like another resource to add to my "self-help toolbox."* Plus, we would have George trapped for seven hours in the car with more time to explore philosophy and Eastern Spirituality.

He shared more about the lineage of meditation Masters from India, and suggested additional books by Swami Muktananda, or Gurumayi Chidvilasananda, the sole head and spiritual master of the Siddha Yoga lineage. During our lunch break, Dave and I strolled down one of the iconic streets of Philadelphia. It's a collection of blocks known for Philly Cheesesteaks, art, and eclectic shops. We were looking for a bookstore called Garland of Letters. The store window looked promising, with spiritual books from all over the world. Entering the room full of tapestries, pictures of Saints and Masters from all traditions, and the aroma of incense, transported me to another place and time. Not finding any of the books George suggested, we approached the counter to inquire. A young fellow with intense eyes, a mischievous smile, and brightly colored scarf around his neck, asked how he could help. We told him what we were looking for, and his response was curious. "Who are you and why do you want to know?" Dave and I turned to look at each other, wondering what had we gotten ourselves into. The book clerk reached under the counter and showed us his well-worn personal copy of *Play of Consciousness,* one of the books we were looking for. He was very familiar with the Siddha Yoga Meditation Path our friend George had described.

"Wow, you've been to India?" we inquired. "Not yet," he replied. "I've been to the meditation and retreat center here in the states for courses, meditation sessions and chanting programs."

We shared our experience watching the chanting video, and our dream to go to India. "Actually, Gurumayi is in residence this summer in her Ashram in Upstate New York." The chance to meet a living master and spiritual teacher here in the states, was beyond our wildest dreams. We had left New Jersey and traveled to Chicago as newlyweds with the intention of "finding God" and our meaning and purpose in this world. There was no doubt that this serendipitous meeting with the book clerk was an important next step in our spiritual quest.

Thanking the bookstore clerk profusely, we purchased the recommended books, tucked them into my backpack, and hurried back to the hotel to tell our friends. Seemed like divine intervention to us. During our lunch break, we met a bookstore clerk, who happened to know the same Spiritual Teacher we had seen on video just days earlier, and was working the day we happened to be in Philadelphia for a Hawaiian spirituality workshop! It certainly appeared the universe had a master plan better than anything I could have imagined.

George made a few calls to friends who had been residents of the Ashram, and as "luck" would have it, his good friend Samantha was still living in-residence. With her help, we scheduled a visit a few weeks later, which happened to be my birthday weekend. During the drive, I vacillated between excitement and amazement. Everything had come together so effortlessly. It was as if the universe had a master plan and we had just shown up and followed the clues. No doubt something big was on the horizon.

The Ashram reception area was buzzing with guests from all over the world. Dave stayed in the check-in line, while I explored the upper lobby and hallways. There were pictures I recognized from the little book store in Philadelphia. Statues representing the great Saints and Teachers from many traditions were visible along the garden paths. Everyone was welcoming, greeting me as if I were a long-distance relative returning home. I entered a large room with few chairs and a lots of empty floor space and meditation cushions. I recognized the large framed photographs that graced the walls, and out of nowhere, my eyes filled with tears. There was a sensation best described as gratitude and a knowing that I was in the right place.

In Chicago, my understanding and view of the world had been greatly expanded. Now, twenty years later, it appeared there was another significant doorway to step through. The doorway was culturally very different from anything I had experienced growing up in New Jersey or Chicago. I made my way back to Dave in the reception area.

"I don't know what goes on upstairs. It brought me to tears just being in the room, and in some unexplainable way, feels like coming home."

Dave went upstairs to see what I was talking about. Incredibly, his experience mirrored mine. A chanting program was scheduled that evening in the large meditation hall. The host for the evening program explained how chanting helps calm the mind and enables a person to go within and find a place of stillness and peacefulness. I had a very hectic job traveling and training hundreds of people a year. Mom was physically deteriorating. Being still and peaceful were not familiar states for me! The words I didn't recognize from the chanting video were in the ancient Sanskrit language. The ancient Yogic Masters believed the sounds and vibration were powerful healing tools and a way to experience peace and stillness within. Following the chant, everyone would sit quietly for meditation. Half-way through the chant, the floor felt as if it were shaking. No, my body was vibrating, like an energetic pulsing. Other than trying to figure out what was happening, my mind was uncharacteristically quiet. Chanting did help prepare me for meditation, as thoughts eventually subsided. After the chanting program, we connected with George and Samantha. I wondered if chanting and meditation would work outside the meditation hall? Samantha responded that with practice it would help me connect with my own divine inner guidance/intuition. The next morning, she explained, we would be back in the large meditation hall, for a special chanting and meditation program, and Gurumayi would be joining all of us.

Samantha guided me to my seat. I could sense the anticipation in the air, as thousands of people prepared to chant sacred mantras and meditate together. I whispered to the woman next to me, "This seems to be quite the event." She smiled and said it was a special morning, as the Guru doesn't always attend in person. Fortunately, Samantha had explained to us the night before that we might experience certain emotions coming up to be released. The particular chant we would do contains one hundred and eighty verses from the most ancient sacred texts. Earlier, at breakfast, George had gifted us our own chanting books. I read his inscription while waiting for the program to start:

"Dear found-again friend and fellow traveler on the path! Welcome Home!!" *How did he know that was exactly what I felt yesterday while exploring? I hadn't shared that experience with him.*

A palpable energy filled the hall as the Guru walked into the room. "Walked" was not quite accurate. I had never seen anyone move with such presence and intention; every movement was purposeful. Halfway through the chanting, it was a struggle to keep my eyes open. I was annoyed that here I was in this amazing place, and I was going to miss something important. Later, I realized it was the beginning of meditation. The end of the chant had a particularly beautiful melody with words easy to pronounce. I looked up and saw Gurumayi gazing in my direction. Slipping into meditation moments later, I had an inner vision of dark and heavy chains being released from around my heart. There was a sensation that my heart was finally free. Uncontrollably, tears began to fall, followed by intense sobbing. A deep release was happening. I knew I was safe, and everything was okay. That I was okay!

Samantha had explained earlier that it was possible for emotions to surface as the letting go would release blockages that prevented me from seeing my own divine essence. I had spent years using food and work as numbing agents for feelings I didn't want to face. Through the power of the mantras and a lot of grace, it felt as if many lifetimes of pain had just let go.

Spiritual awakening manifests differently for each person. And it's always exactly what's perfect for that person. Dave had what he described as a unity experience. A sense of oneness with everything and seeing reality in an entirely new light. It was no accident that my mystical experience focused on opening my heart and filling it with unconditional love. I had been abandoned by my birth mother, and raised by a woman who struggled with her own feelings of unworthiness and conditional approval. There would be more revelations to come. Changes were happening during my "regular life." My mind was quieter, my breathing steadier, and in moments of stress, I recognized I was barely breathing.

Sitting comfortably for meditation was an ongoing adventure. I constantly interrupted myself as I shifted from one position to another. On one very auspicious occasion, I had the opportunity to ask Gurumayi about it. I shared that my meditations were often restless, my body uncomfortable. Gurumayi recommended that I practice hatha yoga. It would help me sit comfortably for meditation. I vowed to do it.

My promise was short-lived. Once back home, work travel increased and my attention to yoga gradually decreased. As embarrassing as it is to admit, it took another year before I realized the Guru's words weren't just a friendly suggestion. I purchased a yoga CD from the Ashram, and began practicing in earnest. Work colleagues commented that I was developing patience and seemed less stressed over deadlines. I noticed a new feeling of actually "being in my body," maybe for the first time. Very naturally, I started making better food choices. Not because I should, but because I felt better when I did it. There was a different level of awareness emerging.

Gurumayi had offered me a lifeline into a practice that went way beyond helping me sit comfortably for meditation.

As my body became more open and flexible, so did my mind. A mystical alchemy had begun and this new discovery invited me to explore my own inner world, and find my own source of love and approval. An exploration that would eventually heal and save my life ten years later.

7

"TODAY, I HAVE SEEN THE FACE OF GOD"

"Yesterday I was clever, so I wanted to change the world.
Today I am wise, so I am changing myself."

—Rumi

We continued to go to the Ashram for special programs and meditation intensives to deepen our understanding. During the summer of 1995, we heard about a volunteer opportunity in India, called The PRASAD Project, an independent not-for-profit organization committed to improving the quality of life of economically and disadvantaged people around the world. It is the philanthropic expression of the Siddha Yoga mission. Dave and I were both moved by their work and how they partnered with the local teams in India to provide medical care in the surrounding villages. In those days, the villagers that lived in the Tansa Valley had very limited access to medical care. Due to the lack of clean water, nourishing food, and protective eye wear, many people, even at ages as young as 35, suffered from cataracts. Because they had no access to medical intervention many would eventually go blind, creating enormous strain on the entire family unit, with devastating repercussions. As resources became available, teams of people from The PRASAD Project India (Prasad means blessing in Sanskrit) would be joined by a worldwide volunteer network to come together and sponsor the Netrapakash Eye Camp. "Light of the eye" is the English translation; they would provide cataract surgeries, eye glasses, and treatment for eye infections at no cost to the patients.

There was significant "on the ground" preparation as a dry rice paddy field and machinist building would eventually be converted into a field hospital of patient tents and state-of-the-art sterile operating suites. Dave and I were ecstatic to discover our applications were accepted and we would head to India in January, 1996. We would be staying at the Siddha Yoga Ashram in Ganeshpuri India, a sacred place we had hoped to visit someday. Never having been out of the country, there was a lot to prepare and learn. Fortunately, a logistics team from The Prasad Project helped every step along the way. What no one could have prepared us for were the life-transforming experiences that awaited. I was surprised to discover doubts creeping in and wondered, "Maybe I'm not made of the right stuff to volunteer?" There was no denying the fact that burn- out had manifested while volunteering in Chicago. Fortunately, with just six months of a daily mediation practice, the ability to recognize fears and doubts, along with thoughts my mind was thinking, was a breakthrough. Just because the mind was thinking them didn't make them true. I would soon discover that India offered multiple opportunities to observe my mind's seemingly never-ending judgement and commentary.

The trip was as uneventful as a twenty-two-hour trip can be. The plane landed in the middle of the night, and immediately our senses were bombarded with the overwhelming smell of pollution and diesel fuel. And that was before we entered the terminal in Mumbai. Making our way through a sea of people to find our driver was a preview of what was to come.

Getting out of the city was a bad combination of bumper cars and the Grand Prix. It was 3:00 am and roads were jammed with all types of transportation: oxen and carts, cows, bicycles, scooters, large and small, brightly colored diesel trucks, taxi and cars. They were all going way too fast for the space they occupied. And on the edges, trying to not get run over, were the brave souls, the pedestrians. The driver took us past blocks of people living in cardboard boxes, next to huge piles of rubbish. And they were the fortunate ones, as they had shelter. Others lived on the sidewalk or worse, on the trash heaps. It was heartbreaking and devastating to see. My attention shifted towards our driver as I realized he was heading straight on towards a brightly painted diesel truck. The road out of the city was barely wider than a one car lane. We careened towards what was surely going to be an accident. I closed my eyes and hung on, bracing for the inevitable impact, praying, "Please don't make it bad enough that we need blood transfusions in a country where AIDS was spreading rampantly." Nothing happened. At the last minute, both drivers veered violently away from each other. Evidently, this was a routine game of playing chicken. "Welcome to India," I said to Dave. I needed to get my nerves under control or it was going to be a very long ride out to the Ashram where we would be staying for the Eye Camp. I pulled my journal from the backpack and captured the first of many insights to remember.

#1: I can't control everything that happens in my life. I can only control my response. And when all else fails, close your eyes and hang on.

We arrived at the gates of the Ashram as the early morning prayers and chants were beginning. Crossing through the metal gates decorated with beautiful painted lotus flowers, we were greeted by the aroma of jasmine flowers and fresh mountain air. Paths curving through the gardens were lined with fruit and flowering trees. After the long plane ride and harrowing road journey, it felt like we had been dropped into paradise. The dorm rooms were simple and comfortable. Most impressive was the wonderful way each person was greeted by the welcoming committee at 4:30 in the morning. Just being in their presence melted my tiredness and stress from the journey.

The second entry in my journal to remember back home.

#2: Greeting people with love and respect matters. It communicates our inherent worthiness, and creates a web of connectedness and acceptance.

We unpacked and took a welcomed nap. Anxious to discover our seva assignments (seva is a Sanskrit word for selfless service), after a delicious breakfast we visited the Volunteer Office. I was hoping to be where the action was, out at the Eye Camp, which was several miles up the road from the Siddha Yoga Ashram. Dave didn't care where his assignment was, just happy to be there. How did he manage to get to that state already? Clearly, I had not mastered accepting that everything happens for the best! The patients weren't scheduled to arrive for another two weeks and much of the work was readying the Eye Camp site. Odds were in my favor. To my dismay, my assignment was nowhere near the

Eye Camp. It was within the Ashram walls. Specifically, cleaning stairways with a small team of people in one of the dining hall buildings.

"This is far worse than anything I had imagined," I muttered to myself. Not only was I not at the Eye Camp, a completely inept supervisor was assigned to the team. Her instructions were to start at the bottom of the stair well and work up. Which of course was illogical, as it meant dirtying the steps, just scrubbed. Grumbling through most of the scrubbing, only to discover at morning break, Dave had a similar assignment in another building. I should have been happy to find him genuinely content. Not so much. Instead of being inspired by his approach, I was annoyed by his calm demeanor. I didn't stay long and retuned to my scrubbing.

Fortunately, the time went quickly. I finished the assignment and began collecting the cleaning supplies. Looking down at my brand-new blue pants, I noticed white spots dotting the fabric from my knees to my ankles. "Something like bleach without the smell must have been in one of the bottles," I exclaimed out loud. Thanks to my inept supervisor, my new pants were ruined. This was not how I envisioned my experience in India going. People at the Ashram in the states who had been to India described their experience as blissful and happy. Obviously, I was not in bliss or remotely happy!

Dave found me sitting on the curb outside still fuming. He was excited to share his next assignment. Evidently, when the logistics team had reviewed his application and discovered he was a scientific glassblower, the perfect job for him immediately came to mind. They assumed he didn't mind heat, and knew how to operate equipment. His assignment would be running the autoclave; a critical apparatus that would sterilize surgical instruments used during the cataract surgeries. Dave approached the autoclave room to begin his training with apparatus expert Prakash. What he saw made him stop dead in his tracks. The autoclave was a large, silver cylinder, with a hand-painted sign hanging overhead. Just weeks before leaving home, Dave had a vivid dream. In the dream he saw Lord Hanuman, one of the most beloved Hindu deities and divine monkey companion of the god Rama sitting cross-legged inside a large silver cylinder.

Hanuman is one of the central characters in the Hindu epic, *Ramayana,* and represents loyalty, service and devotion. Dave's dream reoccurred multiple times, and Dave never understood its significance, until now. The team had lovingly named the silver autoclave Hanuman.

Prakash explained with all its idiosyncrasies, the ancient autoclave never failed them. Incredibly, the scene from Dave's dream weeks earlier was playing out right in front of him. What made this even more perfect was the similarity in the way Hanuman is depicted and Dave's way of being. Like Hanuman, Dave was always ready to help someone in need, and never sought the spotlight. Since becoming friends in high school, he's been a loving supporter through my challenges, as well as an accountability partner when I was out of balance. It was poetic that his assignment with Hanuman, preparing the instruments for the early morning procedures, occurred mostly in the dark of night. Only day two in the Ashram, and already we were experiencing "coincidences and unexplained phenomena" in the sacred and high vibrational atmosphere of the Ashram. The genuine excitement I felt for Dave for his dream assignment descended back into frustration as I showed him my bleach-spotted pants. He was manifesting from his dreams, and I was stuck at the Ashram scrubbing floors with ruined pants. Dave listened compassionately, and quietly suggested, "Why don't you take a walk and change the prescription of your glasses!" I didn't like it, and knew he was right. Walking the garden paths minutes later, feeling the fresh air on my face, the birds singing in the trees, and the incredible floral aromas, the third pearl of wisdom became obvious.

#3: The mind is a powerful tool. It can make you miserable or happy. The choice is mine.

Back from my walk I found a bench outside the main dining hall to rest and appreciate the beauty all around me. A woman walking quickly along the path stopped abruptly when she saw me. "Are you a painter?" she asked. I was perplexed by her question until I realized she was pointing to my pants.

"Ahh, the bleach spots must look like white paint splatters," I said under my breath. "I've painted my share of walls," I responded.

She proceeded to offer me the gift I had been seeking since arriving for the Eye Camp.

"Would you be interested in going out to the Eye Camp to paint the furniture that we will be using in the Operating Rooms and Medical Recovery Tents? Everything needs to be cleaned and painted white. The work has to begin today to meet our deadlines."

Barely able to contain my excitement, I jumped up and gave her a hug. Being amidst the action out at the Eye Camp had been my dream since arriving. I set off to find Dave to share my good news. He nodded with amusement, reminding me that "everything is always working out for the best." Undeniably, trust was not one of my strengths. The new assignment was everything I had hoped it would be. Watching the hundreds of volunteers convert the dry rice paddy fields and factory showroom into a Medical Facility was a masterclass in planning and communication. Threads of different languages and cultures from all over the world were being woven together into a magnificent tapestry. Soon, there would be patients that would experience the intentional effort, love and grace created just for them.

The Eye Camp had planned for five thousand patients overall for the month it would be up and running. Patients would be triaged by need, some receiving glasses, others treatment for their eye infections. The cataract patients would receive a lens implant after cataract removal. There were many moving pieces, and volunteers arrived daily. Opening day approached, and twinges of doubt about my ability to handle everything played in the back of my mind.

I was assigned to Tent One, where initial patient assessments would occur. We would use a simple eye chart to determine next steps for that particular patient. Dave was assigned to Tent Two, where optometrists used equipment to match patients with the right eyeglass prescriptions. Another team of doctors and nurses would evaluate the eye infections and provide the necessary treatments. Two days before opening day, we opted to walk to the Eye Camp instead of taking the converted yellow school bus. During the several-mile walk, we saw people of all ages, some with little hard-sided old-fashioned suitcases, others with just a clothes bundle, walking out of the forests, across fields and dirt roads to make their way towards the Eye Camp. The villagers and farmers set up makeshift camps near the entrance to be ready. They only had to meet one requirement: to be accompanied by a helper escort. This was especially critical for the cataract patients, during their recovery. We watched in stunned silence as children as young as six years of age guided their blind family member through the fields. Most of the patients were farmers from the surrounding villages. For the family to survive, everyone had a role in working the land. If a family member became blind from cataracts, the impact to the entire family's quality of life was significant. Sadly, for some families, the only person they could spare as a helper escort was one of the children. Our teenage translators reported that some of the patients and their escorts had walked four hundred miles to receive care. Word had spread through the Tansa Valley that an Eye Camp offered by the Prasad Project India staff was happening. They trusted their experiences with the medical staff from the Mobile Bus, and knew they would not be turned away. I made a silent vow to stop complaining about the minor inconveniences in my life back home.

A breathtaking kaleidoscope of colors greeted us as the sun rose over the mountains, opening day. Hundreds of us boarded the buses in early morning shifts, united by a common purpose: the heartfelt desire to offer independence and the chance to thrive with medical intervention and compassionate care. The front gate of the Ashram was surrounded by well-wishers from the nearby town of Ganeshpuri. Garlands of orange and yellow flowers were placed over our heads and blessings offered for the day. "Could this day possibly get any better?" I wondered. The buses maneuvered through the village streets and out into the countryside. I pressed my face against the glass to imprint the scene unfolding before me to memory. There was a sea of humanity pouring out from the fields onto the road that led to the Eye Camp. Women in brightly colored saris, men in tan or white colored thin silk shirts and pants, children holding hands, all moving together towards a promise of a brighter future. Tears stained our faces; hearts filled with appreciation for the chance to be part of something much bigger than ourselves.

Pulling onto the dirt field at the edge of the camp, I could see Tent 1. Sometime in the last two days, a queuing system had been constructed of ropes and poles marking a serpentine line. It made for a surreal Disney World feel. All similarities with western culture ended there. The queue line began to fill while our orientation supervisor explained the various roles in our tent. I discovered quickly the most critical part of the team were the young translators from the area school. My post was the initial vision assessments, which appeared to be a well-organized process. First step was to ask the patient to step forward to the line, cover each eye, and identify the objects on the eye chart. My assigned translator would assist in all communications. "How hard could this be?" I thought, as early concerns faded. I smiled, motioning for our first patient to come forward. To my amazement, about twenty people stepped forward. It was at this point I recognized the concept of lines was not something the patients had experienced before. Everything was new for them as it was for us. Naturally, they were curious about what was going to happen. It was a leap of faith coupled with hope that brought them to us. This realization helped shift the focus off my control concerns to how I could welcome them and ease *their* concerns. This noble intention lasted a couple of hours, until at 10:00 am on the dot, our teenage translators announced they were going on chai break.

"All together?" I asked. "Can't you go in shifts so I have coverage?"

"No ma'm, we go as a group with our friends," was the united response. It was clear I was not going to change their process.

I envisioned being asked to leave my post for endangering patient safety as reports of chaos erupting in Tent 1 spread throughout the well-organized camp. Thinking quickly before being totally abandoned, I asked for some key words in the villager's native tongue that I could jot down and reference.

"Welcome, please come forward, line, backup, and stop," seemed most essential. I had a leg up on "thank you" as it looked like the traditional greeting from yoga class, with palms placed together as the unifying greeting of 'Namaskar' was offered: "The light in me honors the light in you."

Taking a deep breath, I realized it was way past time to give up my control issues! Chaos did not erupt. Instead, a fun, party atmosphere ensued as they seemed to find my sorry excuse for speaking Mahrati endearing. The translators returned as promised, and by 5:00 PM all our Tent 1 patients had triaged successfully to Tent 2 for eye glasses and treatment for any eye infections. The cataract patients had progressed to Tent 3, where they would receive a more thorough evaluation and preparation for their surgery.

Dave came over to visit from Tent 2, as I was cleaning up my station. "You have to come over here and check out this Dr. Paul from Canada. He's been seeing patients since this morning using the refractometer to match glasses to their eye condition. He's as loving and patient now as when we started eight hours ago," Dave said.

I was witnessing a real-world example of someone being fully present in the moment. Dr. Paul gently bowed as he said Namaskar to the next patient in line and motioned for them to come forward and take a seat. I chuckled recognizing that the line concept hadn't magically improved in Tent 2. Multiple patients and escorts surrounded the person sitting in the chair, curious to see what the machine on the table was all about. What set Dr. Paul apart was his laser focus on the person immediately sitting in front of him. He seemed able to tune out all distractions and be fully present with the person in front of him. He completed his examination as he had started, bowing and offering the greeting "Namaskar." As the next person began to move forward with their accompanying entourage, he repeated the process. What was most extraordinary? It was as if he had just sat down and was welcoming his first patient. Except this was after eight hours and hundreds of patients later. No wonder his patients seemed less anxious. His face radiated calm compassion. "Remarkable, right?" Dave said. There was no doubt each person in Dr. Paul's presence felt love and respect. It was an inspiring experience to witness and something I vowed to practice.

#4: Being fully present in the moment allows us to welcome every person with love and respect. Namaste, is more than a yoga class greeting. It's a way of honoring who we truly are.

During dinner, we were informed that the number of patients on day one had exceeded the total number anticipated for the entire Eye Camp. The volunteer teams had triaged and taken care of 5,000 patients! Walking through the camp to head back to the bus, we saw many patients sitting together, amazed that their new glasses were allowing them to see again. This group would leave in the morning to go back to their villages. About 1,000 patients, plus their escorts, were resting in the patient care tents, awaiting the next phase of care…lens replacement cataract surgery. Our cataract patients ranged in age from 35 years old to 80. Many patients were totally blind with cataracts in both eyes. The surgeons would only operate on one eye at the camp with plans to operate on the other eye at a later date. For those patients scheduled for surgery at the camp, they would need pre-and post-op care. And to my absolute joy, my next volunteer assignment was working in a new tent with the first group of surgical patients. Our surgeons would begin the surgeries the following day, and our patients in Tent A were the first to be prepped and then monitored post-surgery.

Weaving my way through the maze of giant tents offered a full sensory experience. Every color of the rainbow was represented as patient's colorful sari cloths were gently placed on the ground between the tents, drying in the sun. Our guests had discovered the camp water source. There was a beautiful melodic chant playing over the outside speakers, while the evening meals were being prepared. A rich aroma of cardamom and curry filled the air. Entering Tent A, my new home for a few days, patients and their escorts lining the pathways smiled and bowed, hands clasped together on their hearts as I passed by. Their appreciation was overwhelming and my eyes filled with tears. Wiping them away, I began to fully take in the scene surrounding me. There was a nurse's station at the front of the giant tent, and the floor was lined with mattresses, sheets, pillows and blankets, all placed in neat piles and rows. Our tent held about 300 people – 150 patients and their helpers. There was an expectant and celebratory vibe as patients and their helpers were escorted to their new care spaces. Small gatherings were already forming as patients met their new tent neighbors. Those who spoke English helped explain what would happen the next morning.

Early the next morning, the first pre-op procedure included thoroughly washing the faces of the patients having surgery in the next few hours. There is something so intimate about washing another person's eye and face that left me transformed. There were moments where my hands seemed to disappear, and the hands caressing the patient's face were God's hands, comforting each person. I had no explanation for what was happening. Later in meditation, I realized my feeling of separateness and individualism had disappeared, replaced with the recognition that this person was also me. A new feeling, a sense of oneness, began to emerge during my time at the Eye Camp. Along with the realization that there is only one language...the language of love and compassion.

Following the patients' surgeries, my role was to take their blood pressure and deliver medicated eye drops to reduce the chance of infection and enhance healing. A statistic that astounded all of us, after the Eye Camp was over... *zero* infections or complications in the 1,000 patients who had cataract surgery. This was nothing short of miraculous considering the conditions. Surgeries were conducted in a former machine factory showroom, post-op care consisted of mattresses on a tent floor. Patients were transported between the tents and the Operating Room in old wheel chairs, across rutted dirt paths. The medical staff was not a well-oiled machine, with years of operating together. The doctors, nurses and anesthesiologists were a collective from across the globe. They collaborated and shared their most effective techniques for fast and effective cataract removals, while decreasing infection rates. Science and spirituality merged together and reaffirmed for me the power of healing intention and divine grace.

I met the last morning in Tent A with a twinge of sadness. During the past week, my heart had become so full and expanded, I worried that it would start to close down once I left the camp. *Is this as good as it gets? Is it possible to live in this state?* This last day was about to deliver more inner insight, joy and contentment than all my prior life experiences combined.

When my fellow nurse's aides and I arrived at our station to receive our patient assignments for the day, we discovered a collection of Indian coins (rupees) on the counter. The night nurse explained that when she had returned from her rounds, the offering had been collected by our patients. Most of our patients had only the clothes on their backs and some didn't even have the standard Indian footwear of rubber flip flops, after traveling hundreds of miles through forests and mountain paths. Their gesture of generosity and gratitude for the staff moved each of us to tears. This reaffirmed what I had heard from prior volunteers before leaving the states, yet hadn't fully understood until now. Initially, they too thought they were traveling half way around the world to help people in need. Instead, they discovered it was the patients who healed and transformed them. I asked myself, how is this possible in a country where the poverty hurts so bad sometimes, the only escape is to close your eyes? Yet, here at the Eye Camp, surrounded by people with very little material possessions, there were no hardened hearts or poverty of spirit.

Incredibly, the most unforgettable moment of the Eye Camp was still to come.

Our tent had one of the youngest cataract patients, a man in his mid-30s from a neighboring village. He came to us with cataracts in both eyes, totally blind. Hearing about the Eye Camp, the family made the decision to have their youngest daughter escort and help him. Everyone else was needed on the farm. The young girl walked hundreds of miles, guiding her blind father every step of the journey. Hopes were high that he would regain his sight at the Eye Camp. The patient's eye bandage was scheduled to be removed during afternoon rounds with the doctor. I joined a small group of nurses and aids, gathered around him and his daughter. The surgeon gently removed his bandage, the air filled with anticipation, as he slowly opened his eye. His gaze turned upwards taking in the scene around him. His young daughter, who was kneeling beside him, gently squeezed his hand. Turning towards her, his expression suddenly changed. Amazement and absolute joy radiated from his face as a huge smile appeared. His daughter, Tulsi, had been born seven years earlier, after his second cataract had formed. For the past seven years, he had been totally blind, unable to see his daughter's face... until now.

He alternated between hugging her tightly, drawing back to look into her face, and looking at all of us with amazement. He later explained he wondered if he was dreaming and if she were an illusion that would vanish. Tears flowed freely as we bore witness to this miracle. When he eventually released his daughter, he turned towards all of us. We were crouched on the ground encircling him and his young daughter. Bringing his hands together in front of his heart he looked into each of our faces with heart-opening gratitude.

Bowing, he said, "Today I have seen the face of God."

There is a saying attributed to Black Elk, Medicine Man for the Oglala Sioux: "Today is a good day to die." This is the best way I can express what I felt moving through the camp as I walked out of Tent A for the last time. There was a sense of no regrets or dreams left to fulfill. An unfamiliar sensation starting in my heart and radiating out in all direction began to emerge. Santosha is a beautiful Sanskrit word which means contentment. Peacefulness and contentment inhabited a place I hadn't visited often up until now, and looked forward to exploring. I offered a prayer that I might find my way back to this profound state after leaving the Ashram and Eye Camp.

Mercifully, answers emerged in the days ahead as I began to understand the life-changing experiences. I had gone to the Eye Camp expecting to help others in need. It was becoming evident that the transformational experiences created an opening to new levels of awareness. Doubt was replaced with an inner knowing that the flame ignited inside my heart would be impossible to extinguish. And, the recognition that everything happening around me was ultimately beneficial for my life would become a touchstone for the rest of my life.

This is the last entry in my journal from India.

#5: Love, compassion and respect transcend religion, culture, and language. Oneness is our path back to peace; a place we never left. Finding the way back is as close as the next breath.

A Healing Journey

8

A PROMISE KEPT

"Authenticity is the daily practice of letting go of who we think we're supposed to be and embracing who we are."

—Brene' Brown

I have come to believe that life is a journey of discovery that looks like an upward spiral. Much like a hawk soaring in a thermal current of air. It seems that themes and experiences come back around, almost like a test to see how you might react *this* time. And each time the lesson appears, often with a new face or situation, it somehow gets easier to see the truth of the matter. Until that thing that really bothers you no longer has any hold. There's a letting go of what used to control us. I had been concerned about my ability to "handle" the pressures of the Eye Camp, after my burnout and sense of failure in Chicago. This volunteer experience felt completely different. Life seemed to flow much easier when I let go of a certain outcome. Almost as if there was more space and ease for something even better to happen. I came to the conclusion that there was nothing wrong with us when we were volunteering in Chicago. I was young, idealistic, and believed I alone knew what was right for the world. This set up a constant state of struggle. Ten years later, India taught me that there is grace *and* effort, along with a flowing joy that is possible. While obvious now, the only thing I ever had control over was my response to what happens. Surrendering and releasing rigid expectations provides the ultimate freedom, as expectations rob us of experiencing happiness in the present moment. Not to mention, companions like fear and anxiety tend to tag along when one strays too long in the future. I kept my ruined spotted pants from the Eye Camp as a reminder of how things were always working out for me. Just maybe not in the way I expected!

While in India, I had wondered if I would continue to have insights and progress outside the sacred atmosphere of the Ashram. Surprisingly, one of the first things I noticed was the volume of negative self-talk. I was stunned by the litany of internal criticism and wondered how this crazy person had taken residence in my head. And how had I not noticed her before?

It was clear the next step in my journey of self-awareness was rooting out limiting thoughts, habits, and behaviors. Fortunately, the eating disorder had faded away as my yoga practice deepened. Yoga was helping me live inside my body in a way I hadn't experienced before. I also became aware that as my career advanced so did my long hours away from home. I rationalized this was the price to pay for success, especially being a woman within a predominantly male leadership team. Yet, in moments of quiet, I could hear a challenging inner voice say, "Are you staying busy to avoid something or prove something? Has work become your new eating disorder? Why are you still triggered by your mom?"

A trusted friend suggested a personal development program called The Forum. The approach originated from the EST trainings done by Werner Earhart. It involved leaving your "normal" life for a long weekend and moving beyond limiting beliefs to create a new world of infinite possibilities. I was intrigued with anything that would help me drop limiting beliefs and step into my full potential. Which I identified years later as code for "be happy!" The workshops were held in a downtown Boston hotel. As two hundred people settled in for the long weekend, our facilitator came onto the stage, lugging a kitchen stool on his back. He turned toward all of us and asked, "Who here is ready to let go, and go beyond their story?" He had my attention. *Could this weekend help heal my relationship with my mother?*

Curiously, my biggest breakthrough that weekend came from the assignment to write out our life story. We were to capture the recurring themes that we played over in our minds and complained about. We were instructed to find a partner, and read our complete story out loud to that person, and then switch. The next step was to find nine other people and repeat the process. *Seriously? My story is about 10 pages, front and back. It is exhausting repeating it once.* By the fifth person, I was sick and tired of telling my story. I couldn't help but notice it focused on all the slights and wrongs I had ever experienced. The facilitator asked us to consider how our retelling of the story kept us trapped as victims, unempowered and doomed to re-live themes that no longer served us. Could we envision re-writing the story or even better, thanking it for the insights and experiences provided? And then release the story and its ability to control our future?

I recognized that much of what the instructor was teaching was aligned with the practice of yoga. He offered a new visceral experience that helped me connect the dots in a different way. As the weekend unfolded, I became even more aware of the seemingly never-ending commentary going on in my mind, masquerading as a trusted friend. No wonder I had eaten and exercised my way through the challenging times in my life. I was trying to find some quiet and peace. Fortunately, the facilitator threw out a life-line.

"Now that you are aware of the inner critic, you have the choice to think a different thought."

He offered an interesting approach that proved effective as it put me into the role of detached observer.

"Thank your inner critic for their unsolicited opinion. Let them know you are choosing to move on without them."

The most humbling element of his suggestion was the realization of how much my "inner critic" had to say… about everything! Fortunately, two empowering quotes on the whiteboard offered hope for improvement.

"A thought is just a belief we keep thinking."

"Changing beliefs can create health and vitality for the rest of your life."

Later that evening, I vowed that my inner critic's days were numbered. I didn't fully realize that this would be another one of those "life-practices," much like yoga and meditation.

The most enlightening exercise of the weekend came on the last day. It illustrated how interconnected we human beings really are! The facilitator instructed everyone to close their eyes and raise their hand if we had experienced any of following thoughts. "I am a failure." "I'm a fraud." "I'm not good enough." "I'm not enough." "If people only knew the real me." When he asked us to open our eyes, I could not believe what I was seeing. Every hand in the room was raised. Hundreds of people from all over the country, different backgrounds and professions, millionaires and people who borrowed the money to attend. Yet somehow, we all had experienced similar limiting beliefs about ourselves? He shared with us that no matter who facilitates the program, or in what country, the results are always the same. These phrases of unworthiness are universal, and drive many of the ineffective behaviors and coping mechanisms we employ to either drown out or mask our feelings. How we choose to respond is what makes us unique. I had lots to think about on the drive home.

Could it be this was why I had spent so much time trying to be "the best"? Did I fundamentally believe I wasn't enough?

Was this the reason my relationship with my mom was so challenging? Each of us trying to prove "we're ok"?

Fortunately, Dave was also participating in the session and offered welcome support. "Well, this got very real and personal." Dave reassured me that I must be strong enough to handle it or I wouldn't have put myself into the course. My intention had been to root out limiting beliefs and heal my relationship with my mother. It was unclear how the experiences of the workshop were going to play out and help me over the next few months. The answer arrived the following morning. Its impact would be immediate.

I took the Monday after the workshop off from work, to bring my mother to her dentist appointment. During the drive, I shared with her some of the experiences from the workshop. I didn't hold back my experiences and insights. I shared the "Story Exercise" and the sections that related to her that we had never talked about. She was surprised by how many of my childhood memories centered around anger, hurt or fear. For the first time I shared the fear I felt when she dressed me up like a little doll to visit the dark church with the nuns. And how unsettling it had been finding her frantically scrubbing the basement floor like a madwoman, with no explanation. And the terror I experienced the day she packed her bags to leave me and my dad. Trusting she could hear it all, I shared my dismay and anger that she let my dad die alone. And finally, the biggest secret of all: that I had been searching for my birth mother from the time I turned eighteen. How I desperately wanted to know my real ancestry and medical history, yet at the same time, I never wanted her to think I didn't appreciate the life she gave me.

There were lots of tears as she listened without interrupting. It was an incredibly freeing experience that I never thought possible. She was able to provide different perspectives from how my young mind had interpreted what had happened. Apologies were made by both of us. Somehow, The Forum workshop gave me the tools to feel safe expressing what was truly in my heart. And she was able to hear me in a way that didn't threaten her. Judgement dissolved and the only thing present was the recognition that something deep had been healed between us. A few hours later, the significance of this moment would be revealed.

We arrived home around noontime, and Mom settled into her section of the house. I went upstairs to my office to do some paperwork. Thirty minutes later, I was interrupted by the sound of a large crash and moan. I ran downstairs to find my mother helpless on her living room floor. Once the paramedics arrived I called Dave, and told him it was likely a stroke with her history of TIAs. While following the ambulance I recounted the miraculous morning conversation we had earlier. And concluded by saying,

"I don't know if she is going to live, and if she does survive, what her mental condition will be. We may never have another conversation like we had today."

She survived the stroke with paralysis on one side of her body, and limited mental processing ability. While being treated, the physicians discovered she had an abdominal aneurysm. Since she was in her eighties, the risk of surgery outweighed the risk of a rupture. They opted not to intervene, with the expectation that it could leak at some time in the future. Initially, it was on my mind constantly and I wondered if I would be with her when it happened. Mom was a fighter and survivor from when she was a young girl facing death or the possible loss of her legs. I recalled the times I was "insulted" when she told me "I was just like her." Now, I could see it as the compliment she meant it to be. She surprised even her wonderful team of physical therapists with her progress, eventually being able to stand, sit and pivot from her wheelchair into the car. The aneurysm eventually faded into the back of my mind. We were able to find a wonderful nursing home close by. With the physical and mental limitations, I sometimes wondered what was keeping her here. *Was there something she still wanted to experience? Could it be something her condition would teach me?*

On June 12th 2001, the inevitable finally happened. Upon arriving at a hotel in Connecticut for a business meeting, I received a call from my corporate office. They had been notified by a nurse at Portsmouth Hospital in New Hampshire that my mom had been rushed there from the nearby nursing home. I called Dave immediately. I had a five-hour drive ahead of me, and I needed someone on the ground getting answers. I took a deep breath and called the nurse. She explained, "Your mother's aneurysm has started to leak and her only chance of survival is immediate surgery. She is being prepped now." It had been three years since they had found the abdominal aneurysm and I had finally stopped worrying about when it might rupture. "Why are they prepping her for surgery?" I asked. She had been declining steadily the past six months, and I wanted to know who had given the approval for the surgery. I was her Health Care Power of Attorney. The nurse explained that she was still conscious when she arrived at the hospital. It was unlikely she understood what was happening, yet somehow, they decided she had given them the okay to proceed. I went from zero to sixty on the emotional scale and demanded to know how they could make that decision without contacting me first. The nurse said there hadn't been time.

I had a lot of time to think on the five-hour drive north to the hospital. I called Dave every thirty minutes, prepared to hear she had passed away during surgery. She was still in surgery when I pulled into the hospital parking lot. I knew that if she wasn't out of surgery at this point, there had been a major complication. Dave was in the waiting room, and had received zero updates. I sat down and began taking slow, deep breaths to calm the anxiety I was feeling. It seemed like an eternity before the surgeon finally came to talk with us. He had a smile on his face as he approached.

"Good news. She's survived the surgery," he announced. Somehow, I knew there was a but coming. After a short pause he continued, "There was a complication. We had trouble drawing all the abdominal "layers" together, so we inserted a large sheet of Teflon to hold everything together. She's on her way to the Intensive Care Unit, and you can see her soon."

Yogic breathing went out the window as I responded in a very loud voice, "Are you serious? You did your job in keeping her alive, but what type of quality of life is she going to have now? She's already paralyzed, mentally declining, and in a nursing home."

The ferocity of my anger caught me and him by surprise. He visibly winced and stumbled backwards as if struck by an invisible force. Saving lives was what he had been trained to do. His mission was complete.

We found our way to the Intensive Care unit. Mom definitely looked like someone who had just come out of a long, complicated surgery. There were tubes and monitors everywhere. Dave and I held each of her hands and let her know we were there. We stayed until they kicked us out. No matter how much you can anticipate a moment like this, there is no adequate preparation for the actual experience of it. For the next two weeks, I sat with her every day in the ICU. I softly sang the sacred chants and mantras I had learned in India that contained powerful, healing frequencies. There were no indications she was regaining consciousness, yet I was certain she knew I was there. With nothing further able to be done for her in the specialized care unit, she was moved to a regular room. I decided it was time to return to work. About two hours into my first day back, her nurse called to say her breathing had changed, and we should come quickly.

Dave and I met in her new room. The tubes and monitors were all gone. The only medical apparatus was her oxygen mask. And still no sign of regaining consciousness. All we could do was help her be comfortable. We stood on each side of the bed, each of us holding her hand. Since the surgery, I had my chanting book with me at all times. We decided to sing the most sacred text we knew. It had been sung during our first visit to the Ashram on the morning we met Gurumayi. This choice was as much for us as for her. I needed all the spiritual support possible recognizing she would be leaving her body soon. As a medical technology student, I had been in hospital rooms when patients coded and died. The atmosphere was chaotic and impersonal. I wanted Mom's experience to be peaceful and loving.

This chant held significant meaning for many reasons. While singing it for the first time, I had the sensation of heavy chains being released from my heart. It would become a theme for the rest of my life, as many of my transformative experiences had to do with opening my heart and letting love in. The Eye Camp in India, the emotional breakthroughs from The Forum workshop, and years of meditation and yoga; all had taken me on a journey into my heart. And now, here at my mother's side, I had the incredible honor of helping her leave her body. Tears began to fall as I realized that all the past hurts and misunderstandings we experienced were resolved the morning of her stroke, three years earlier. Grace and effort merged and enveloped me in a blanket of love.

As we began to sing, there were times when mom would inhale, and then nothing. No sound of an exhale. The first time it happened, Dave and I stopped singing and looked at each other, asking "Is this it?" It began to happen with more frequency, and at one point, we began to chuckle. A combination of stress relief and wondering if she was just "having fun" with us to lighten the mood.

Her breathing did completely stop as we completed verse 177. Mom left her body on an exhale. I like to think her angels breathed her home. As the chant had progressed, she appeared to become more relaxed and even peaceful. She never showed any signs of pain or distress. I looked down at the verse we had just ended. Through my tears I read aloud the translation. "Repetition of the sacred mantra at the time of death brings liberation. All the actions of a devoted disciple are accomplished everywhere."

Dave and I looked at each other in amazement. "How was this even possible? There are 180 verses and the verse in which she left her body was this one?" I asked.

I leaned over to remove Mom's oxygen mask and kissed her cheek. I was shocked to feel how heavy her head felt. No wonder people use the expression "dead weight." *Did the soul actually make the body lighter?*

Dave motioned to the hospital window near her bed as we sat in silence, allowing the magnitude of what had just happened to settle in. Outside the third-floor window were five dragonflies circling each other. We took it as a sign from Mom, letting us know she was okay.

Later that evening, I looked up the meaning of dragonflies in the book *Animal Speaks*. It suggests that when a dragonfly crosses your path it symbolizes "Change, transformation, and self-realization. The change has its source in understanding the deeper meaning of life."

Well, that certainly seemed appropriate for someone crossing over from this reality and merging into expanded consciousness. I like to think that the five dragonflies represented my father, her two sisters, and her parents, welcoming her home. Years later, while helping my Aunt Footsie make her final journey, a medium emphatically declared "No one passes over alone. A loved one or spiritual figure is always with them." I choose to accept this as truth.

On the way to the funeral home, a mega realization dawned. "Dave, remember the promise that I made after my dad died? That no one in my family would ever die alone again? If the surgeon hadn't performed surgery, and made the decision to keep her alive, she would have died BEFORE I made it to the hospital!"

My mind was racing. *How did I miss this earlier while the surgery was happening? Or later while she was in the ICU?*

I like to believe that my mother was guiding me to this realization from the other side!

I had been angry and ungrateful toward the surgeon. It appeared that once again, the universe seemed to have a better plan than I did. The surgeon, nurses, and my mom, all came together to help me keep a forgotten promise... that no one in my family would ever die alone. A promise that was made twenty-seven years earlier by a heart-broken seventeen-year-old daughter, on the night her father died alone. And Mom, in her dying moment, gave me an invaluable gift. The chance to be with the most important person in my life as she made her final journey. Later that evening, I wrote a heartfelt note to the surgeon thanking him 'for a promise kept.'

Chris, Mom and Dave

9

"YOU DESERVE TO BE HAPPY"

"The only thing that was ever wrong with me was my belief that there was something wrong with me."

—Glennon Doyle

There is subtle shift in awareness many women describe as they enter their fifties. It's the recognition we have finally arrived, and no longer need to justify ourselves. Professionally, I had multiple promotions and had survived a vice president's attempts to fire me because I challenged his aggressive and sexist behaviors. Physically, my journey through menopause had been eased and supported by a Naturopathic Practice that focused on women's health. Our finances were secure, my relationship with Dave was better than ever, and life was good. As a recovering Catholic, I did wonder when the "other shoe would drop." It decided to "hit the floor" just before my fifty-third birthday. I noticed symptoms in late menopause that prompted me to visit the gynecologist. After multiple exams and procedures, the pathology report stated stage 1 uterine cancer. The surgeon in Boston recommended a complete hysterectomy. I knew a lot about this part of the body, having spent most of my career as an immunologist and working in a women's health company. I felt unsettled on the drive home about her recommended treatment for many reasons. It was early stage, I was still experiencing menopausal symptoms, which meant my hormones were "all over the place." As I pulled into my driveway, the essential component of my discomfort was finally identified. I was being asked to make a decision without any medical history.

After the Adoption Agency closed and locked the door years earlier, I was going to have to find a way to pry it back open. I explained my new situation, and they promised to get back to me. I emphasized the surgery was scheduled around the Christmas holidays and time was of the essence. The last time it took the agency 48 hours to call me back with the news that there would be no chance for any communication. I had been rejected yet again. This time it took them four months to break my heart. In the meantime, I put my head down, focused on work, with the accompanying mantra, "Just follow the surgeon's advice and get the surgery done as soon as possible. The sooner you do it, the sooner you can move on with your life."

What I didn't count on was the impact my 14-year yoga and meditation practice would have on my old patterns of behavior. Four days before my scheduled surgery over Christmas, I attended one of my favorite yoga classes in a quaint studio located near the ocean, in Newburyport, Massachusetts. While in the final resting pose, shavasana, something happened that changed my life forever. I had been on a quest to solve my adoption puzzle from the time I turned 18. This unconventional decision would eventually lead to finding the missing piece.

The voice inside my head was loud and so real, I opened my eyes to see who was talking to me in yoga class.

"What do you think you are doing? You've not researched any other options."

The voice continued, "You and Dave have successfully combined western medicine with integrative healing approaches for years. Why are you not using all your resources?"

Stunned, I completed the class, gathered my belongings and sat in the car to absorb what had just happened.

Was this fear about the surgery talking or a message to choose differently? The voice inside my head wasn't done getting my attention, as more questions arose.

What's the hurry? One pathologist reported hyperplasia, the other pathologist called it Stage 1. Who says hyperplasia has to progress to stage whatever, anyway?

What if the uterine cells were going through some "normal" menopausal hormonal changes?

Remember your gut feeling when the surgeon said don't worry… this was the most common surgery done in women your age?

In hindsight, I think the state of deep relaxation I had attained as a result of the yoga class created an opening for my innate wisdom to rise from a place of stillness. It interrupted my programmed pattern of "get it done, move on," and brought to mind Dave's incredible healing experience. Ten years earlier, Dave experienced a reversal of crippling arthritis when he was in his early forties using a holistic and Naturopathic approach. We both believed in the power of the body to heal itself, when the right environment for healing and wellbeing is created. I had direct knowledge, and multiple friends who had experienced sustained healing with a holistic approach after Western Medicine's pharmaceutical model of just treating symptoms had failed them. *But curing arthritis and Crohn's disease were one thing. Did I truly believe it was possible to apply the same approach with cancer?*

I continued to contemplate the message delivered while I was on my yoga mat and decided to slow down, do more research, and ask better questions. A few days after my yoga class, I postponed the surgery and assembled a new health-care team. The path became clearer after consulting with Dr. Beth Devlin, a well-respected Naturopath with an expertise in Women's Health. I became more committed than ever to own my health and healing journey. The journey would include a mind-body-spirit integrative approach. Which meant utilizing western imaging, screening and monitoring technology, coupled with Naturopath healing modalities, and an honest look at my emotional health. As I suspected, my lab results showed significant imbalances and gave us a place to begin the treatment protocol. In addition to hormonal therapies, nutritional and dietary changes, and stress reduction, my medical plan also included biopsy and ultrasounds at prescribed intervals from the surgeon. She had agreed to allow me "several months" to follow this alternative path.

It had been a month since I contacted the Adoption Agency, and still no word. A few nights after cancelling the surgery, I had a dream. The message was clear. That after many failed attempts and rejection, I couldn't rely on the Adoption Agency. I needed to become my own "adoption detective," accelerate my search and solve this mystery. This was not a dress rehearsal; my life depended on it. The last thing I remember before waking up was the phrase, "Use unconventional methods." *What did that even mean?*

My experiences in India had led me to explore paths that presented themselves, and felt right. I shared my dream with a trusted friend, and she recommended a medical intuitive who had worked with Dr. Christiane Northrup. Dr. Northrup, a practicing holistic Obstetrics and Gynecology physician, wrote the groundbreaking book and international bestseller, *Women's Bodies, Women's Wisdom: The Complete Guide to Women's Health and Wellbeing.* I didn't know what a medical intuitive was or what they actually did, yet I trusted Dr. Northup's work. I was about to be totally blown away by what the intuitive offered. Over the phone, she told me I was thirty pounds overweight. This was true. I wouldn't give her any points for finesse, yet I couldn't argue with her assessments. She also told me it was essential that I lose weight as the excess fat was storing estrogen. Beyond what was happening in my uterus, she was concerned about a potential breast cancer manifesting. Without mincing words, she said, "Lose weight now. It will save your life." She also told me I needed to "lighten up." Laughter and dancing were her treatment suggestions. I loved to dance, but hadn't ventured down that road for many years. Work always came first.

In yoga there is a practice called discernment. If something resonates, explore and ask questions. If it doesn't, move on. For me, this was a sticky proposition. It seemed sometimes my fearful worried voice drowned out my inner guidance voice. Meditation and breathing helped. The medical intuitive words resonated and shortly after the consult, while on vacation, a friend introduced me to Zumba! The medical intuitive was right. I did have an inner dancer, and after years of travel and working late into the evenings, she was thrilled to be let out! Halfway through the first song, I began to cry. I heard my inner voice say, "Finally, you get the message that your body is more than a vehicle to hold up your mind." Incredibly, over the next six months, thirty pounds melted off as my metabolism increased and I found child-like joy while dancing. Zumba made me happy. And most curious, one of the few pieces of information I received regarding my birth mother was that she loved to dance!

As part of my integrative approach, I needed to educate myself more about the mind-spirit-body connection. I had read Christiane Northrup's book, *Women's Bodies, Women's Wisdom,* years earlier, and it occupied a revered place on my book shelf. Now, with a particular concern, it was time to take it off the shelf. I studied the section on reproductive health. Dr. Northrop made a statement linking "unresolved grief, sadness, and loss" to the second chakra energy center and reproductive health. I paused to let that sink in. *Who hasn't experienced grief, sadness, and loss at this stage in their lives? Afterall, my dad died when I was in high school. I certainly experienced my share of loss and sadness at an early age.*

I dismissed this section, not recognizing the significance of her words. Her book did convince me to add other healing modalities to my Integrated Health Plan.

As "luck" would have it, a former business colleague Laura Moore, now a board-certified Naturopathic Doctor, Acupuncturist and Asian Medicine Practitioner, moved back to the Seacoast area to begin her practice. Her holistic approach to transforming imbalances into health included a sound-healing modality utilizing tuning forks. The tuning forks are calibrated to vibrate at certain frequencies. The practitioner determines the appropriate areas and patterns that promote healing and rebalance the body. This became my favorite healing modality as my body readily absorbed the healing frequencies. Dr. Moore was an answer to a prayer. She was the exact medical expert I needed in my life at the exact right time. Everything was open to being shifted and healed, and I trusted her as she attended to my whole being: the physical, mental, emotional and spiritual components of me. A feeling of general well-being immediately followed each session, accompanied by gentle emotional releases and insights days later. It became painfully obvious as we worked together that my work habits had gotten "way" out of balance, and my body had suffered. As our work together progressed, I became more attuned to how my thoughts and feelings affected my body. I was uncovering another layer of awareness and intuitive questioning. After one particularly impactful session, I mentioned the passage in Dr. Northrup's book I had dismissed. Dr. Moore suggested it might have more relevance to my current situation than I thought. She encouraged me to be open and explore what that might be.

A few weeks later, a yoga colleague made a statement that captured my attention. "You know, you *deserve* to be happy." It's funny how a simple statement can trigger a search for honest answers. It reminded me of the time I was deep in the throes of a challenging relationship with my mother, and the NLP practitioner said,

"You know you aren't responsible for her happiness. You aren't responsible for anyone else's happiness."

His comment became the catalyst that allowed me to finally drop resentment and find compassion and forgiveness...for me and my mother. And now more questions about happiness, although this time, it was more personal.

Am I not happy?

The word deserve is really strong. Is happiness a right or something I'm responsible to create?

What does this have to do with my current medical situation?

These questions could not be swept under the rug. I brought them into my next session with Dr. Moore. What surfaced after very deep healing work took me totally by surprise. And to a place where I felt safe enough with Dr. Moore's help to explore some very dark spaces.

All the emotional blocks I had stacked and hid behind for much of my life, were they all connected to being adopted?

Was it possible that being adopted had set up a lifetime of suppressed feelings about unworthiness?

I had blamed my mother for pushing me "to be perfect." But was it a pre-determined situation necessary to teach me that I never had to prove myself worthy of love and happiness?

Forget happiness and love. I had been abandoned as a newborn baby. For my entire life, had I been desperately trying to prove my very right to exist?

These questions demanded some serious introspection and might take a while! As strange as this may sound, I hadn't connected being adopted with my past or present emotional state and current health situation. Since junior high I had focused solely on finding medical information and ancestry. I had heard stories of adopted children finding out they were adopted in high school or as adults, and how it set them into a tailspin. They felt as if their whole lives had been a lie. I took pride in being well-adjusted, knowing from a very young age that I was adopted. Even special, as my parents 'picked me,' over all the other children. I was starting to think I had been running from the real possibility that if "they picked me," then they could change their mind and "return me!"

During my next healing session, I consulted my journal relaying to Dr. Moore the ongoing insights emerging during the past few weeks. A deeply buried memory from the last time I had tried to find my birth mother back in 1994 had surfaced. It had been 20 years since my first attempt and would be my fifth and final attempt. The final attempt, more devastating than all prior attempts as it was a confirmation of abandonment, unworthiness and rejection. Dr. Moore listened intently as I relayed the specifics.

"The social worker from the Adoption Agency agreed to be my intermediary and called the last phone number on record for my mother. She reached a woman who was "speaking on my mother's behalf." The woman was curt, explaining that I was a secret no one in the family knew about. She refused to accept a letter or pictures from me. Her message clear: "still not wanted."

I explained to Laura that the saving grace were the clues offered by the social worker as she tried to soften another rejection. And that in preparation for the social worker's call, I had researched articles on doing adoption searches. The articles emphasized two things: writing everything down and keeping the notes in a safe place, *and* the importance of listening with your "whole being." It was possible that a social worker might "accidently" drop clues that would become significant later on. Fortunately for me, I did find a sympathetic social worker who offered the following pieces of information:

My birth mother lived on a farm somewhere on the Ohio or Kentucky border.

She had seven children and did not drive.

Her father had been killed tragically in a boat explosion sometime around 1974.

Her first name was either Mildred or Lois.

Unfortunately, there was no updated medical information or ancestry. I hung up the phone, and for months considered hiring a detective. After much deliberation, I went into my heart, and put myself in my mother's shoes. Maybe this secret would destroy her marriage? Or ruin her relationship with her children? So, I made the very difficult decision to let go of the idea of ever finding peace and closure with her. This time, when I closed the door and sealed it shut, I believed it was my mother's wish. The Adoption Agency agreed this was for the best.

Retelling this story, in the winter of 2010, sparked a new revelation. It had now been five months since my diagnosis, and I was on the verge of confronting another truth about my search attempts. I looked at Dr. Moore with tears in my eyes.

"Is it possible my searches were never just about finding medical information and ancestry? Even the search I just re-ignited? I just couldn't admit it to anyone. Not even to myself."

For the first time I was able to see the benefits of an integrated healing journey. As we worked on healing my physical and emotional body, I was becoming *strong enough to dive into the pain and examine the truth. And the truth was "setting me free."*

There was one part of the story that kept bothering me as I drove home that night. *Who was the woman speaking on my mother's behalf?* I recalled asking the social worker, and her response had been an "older woman" who declined to identify herself. I dropped all subsequent attempts to find my birth mother based on an unidentified woman, speaking on her behalf. That night as I drifted off to sleep, I realized this latest question seemed newly relevant to my current search efforts and demanded further exploration.

A trusted friend suggested I consider past life regression therapy as it could help me gain clarity into the situation. It seemed like a stretch to me, not to mention I didn't know anyone in the field. Days later, in what can only be described as a magical and synchronistic encounter, I found myself at a gathering, in a conversation with a therapist who used hypnosis and past-life regression as healing modalities in her practice. The dream I had months earlier had suggested I use "unconventional methods." This certainly qualified as the most unconventional method I had considered. Curious, and rationalizing I had nothing to lose, I decided to schedule an appointment. The experience proved frustrating, unsettling, and enlightening. Most importantly, it reaffirmed my decision to do whatever it took to find my birth mother before any rescheduled surgery.

10

INVITATION TO HEAL

"In order to change your life outside, you must change inside.
The moment you are willing to change, it is amazing how the
universe begins to help you. It brings you what you need."

—**Louise Hay**

S pending my career as an immuno-virologist or training
director in a medical device organization, things I
could see and measure were familiar territory. My
healing journey was sending me on unexpected paths, where
"logical" explanations were replaced with synchronicities
and mystical occurrences.

This next path would be one of the most intriguing.
Dr. Lyons explained the process involved with past-life
regression therapy as a mix between guided meditation and
hypnosis. I felt comfortable with the process she explained
and curious about would happen next. After about twenty
minutes of quiet relaxation, I began to feel agitation. I was
not seeing or getting any answers in response to Dr. Lyon's

questions. Just a blank slate and wall of silence. Until she asked this question: "Is there someone who is blocking you from the information you are seeking?" Slowly, a detailed image came into view. In front of me was a square metal box, reinforced with rivets, about the size of a toolbox. It was old and rusty. Encasing it were thick chains, secured by a padlock with a place to insert a skeleton key. I saw myself trying unsuccessfully to break the chains. An old woman's face appeared, and finally I had an answer to her question.

"My grandmother. She is the one that is keeping the secret about me locked in the box, not my birth mother. It's never been my birth mother." There were also strange and unexplained images of black and white cloth dolls similar to things I'd seen in museums circa the 1800s. In the final moments of the session, images of my life as a Native American woman came into view on the screen of my mind. They included some very disturbing scenes and I abruptly ended the session. I had no intention of re-living past trauma or having dark memories released. However, I did find it fascinating that a Native life emerged, given my unexplained connection to Indigenous cultures.

"Was there any value in the past-life regression session?" Dave inquired when I met him in the lobby downstairs.

"Surprisingly, yes. Remember when I had promised to 'honor' my birth mother's secret years ago, and very reluctantly broke that promise after my cancer diagnosis? Well, after what seemed like an eternity, an image and clear message came through. It had been my grandmother speaking to the social worker on my mother's behalf!" I paused to let the revelation sink in.

"And not only that, there was a message that my grandmother did *not* have my mother's blessing to speak for her. In fact, just the opposite. My mother is as interested in finding me as I am in finding her. You know it's been four months since I called the Adoption Agency asking for their help. I'll give them one more week, and if they still have nothing to offer I will hire a private detective."

Dave leaned over and giving me a reassuring hug, he whispered, "I support your efforts. You've come too far to stop now."

I continued to focus on an integrated healing plan, hopeful there would be changes in the next biopsy. It had been seven months since the initial diagnosis, and four months after postponing surgery. The previous biopsy and ultrasound in mid-April showed no changes, in either direction. I had been hanging onto the hope that the Adoption Agency would get back to me with my mother's medical information before a new surgery date needed to be considered. After multiple unanswered messages to the agency, fear was beginning to wear me down. It was as if I were dangling by a precarious thread, interwoven with healing possibilities, worry and doubt. As a scientist, my sensibilities were constantly challenged, as my heart said "give it more time." The fraying thread eventually broke under the pressure, and I set a new surgery date for mid-May.

The actual date was the Friday before Mother's Day weekend. At the time, I was oblivious to the "guardian, protector and motherhood" themes surrounding me all my life. Now they seemed obvious and illuminating. I had decided not to have children because of the lack of genetic information about potentially carrying the cystic fibrosis gene. Yet, after our wedding, children occupied our apartment in Chicago much of the time. Our weekend nights for seven years consisted of looking after them at the Drop-in center. There were even shared vacations with Good News North of Howard parents and sponsors, as we brought the children to places they had only imagined. Years later, work colleagues on the team commented on how I shielded them from the drama of internal politics, and helped them chart a successful course for their future. Sometimes, to my own peril.

Of course, the obvious yet not so obvious at the time. My birth mother couldn't keep me; my adopted mother went through hell and back to get me; and now I was on the brink of losing major parts of my anatomy which were the very representation of being a woman and a mother.

While traveling to Las Vegas for a business trip, I read the book *Prepare for Surgery, Heal Faster, A Guide of Mind-Body Techniques*. A friend suggested that since the surgery was in a few weeks, why not stack the deck in my favor? The author, Peggy Huddleston, a graduate of Harvard Divinity School, had done extensive clinical research on the power of mind-body techniques to enhance healing. The book outlined five steps to prepare for surgery and included studies from major hospitals in the Boston area. I was very curious about the impact of deep relaxation on the immune system. With the integrated health team assembled months earlier, healing modalities such as aromatherapy, acupuncture, sound healing and hypnosis had expanded my scientific horizons. I devoured the book; every page relevant to my situation. Some patients experienced physical improvement prior to their pre-operative appointments. And all used less pain medication and recovered faster than expected. I found myself mysteriously drawn to Peggy Huddleston's picture. She looked familiar, yet I was certain we hadn't met. I was certain she was going to play a very important role in my healing process. I completed the book as we landed and decided to schedule a consultation once I settled into the hotel.

On the way to baggage claim, a missed call popped up from a New Jersey area code. It was the Adoption Agency calling back after months of waiting. Anxious to know what was going on, I listened to the voicemail while descending on the airport escalator. A woman's voice said,

"We've located your birth mother."

"Oh my god" I said out loud, my heart started racing.

"Unfortunately, she passed away in September."

Instantly, tears burst forth. Doubling over, it was as if I had been hit by an unseen force to my abdomen. Tears turned into uncontrollable sobs as I struggled to catch my breath. The realization that I would never sit with her and discover who she was and if she thought about me was heartbreaking. There would be no happy reunion.

A clear voice inside broke through the pain. *This is the unresolved grief, sadness and loss from Dr. Northrup's book about the second chakra.*

I had never experienced such intense pain. Not even when my father died unexpectedly, when I was just 17. I was breaking apart from the inside as sadness and despair consumed me. Steadying myself against a wall I struggled to gain composure.

Somehow I managed to return the call and reach the woman who had left the message.

"What did she die from?" I asked.

"We don't know," she responded.

"My new surgery date is in two weeks. Knowing she's dead and in her early 70s makes finding cause of death even more critical."

"I understand. But there is no way for us to find out."

"How can that be?" I asked. "It's critically important I know this information. If she died from uterine, ovarian, or breast cancer, the scale and scope of my surgery would change greatly. If you are too busy to do the research, just send me my files. I'll research on my end."

"Oh no," she said. "I can't send the files. It's against the law here in New Jersey. Your adoption files are permanently sealed as New Jersey is a closed state."

*"Are you kidding me? Same **** I heard when I was 18. How is this still the case?"*

I was totally blindsided. It had never occurred to me that even after birth mothers passed away, the files would remain sealed. Fighting back tears of anger, I asked, "How is it right that the law continues to protect the rights of birth mothers who have died?"

"Adoptees have no rights in the state of New Jersey. Your only option is to hire a lawyer, and petition the court for medical reasons."

"How much would something like this cost?"

"Based on prior experiences, somewhere between $20,000 and $30,000. And unfortunately, there is no guarantee that they would open the file," she added.

And that's when I snapped!

"How can you put the rights of a dead woman above mine?" I screamed into the phone. "I am a living, breathing person, facing a surgery with no medical history. And oh, by the way, my mother is dead and we don't know what from?"

The voice on the other end of the phone was sympathetic, however there would be no clues offered this time. There was nothing left to say.

I called Dave to tell him what had just happened and that there was a strong possibility I would postpone the surgery. It was hard to imagine being in the "right emotional state" for surgery in just two weeks. Back at the hotel, and fairly certain I was going to cancel, I decided to call Peggy Huddleston's office anyway. I felt an unexplainable sense of urgency to meet her. Her assistant explained that she would be back in her office for just one day the following Monday, and then out of the country for a couple of months. Without pausing, I told her Monday would work, with no idea where Peggy Huddleston's office was located. Incredibly, her office was fifteen minutes from my office outside Boston. Even this scientist, trained with data and things seen under a microscope, could not ignore the synchronicity presenting itself. Peggy Huddleston was the lifeline I needed. I just didn't understand why yet.

Pushing back my emotions, I had to focus on the business meeting that brought me to Las Vegas. People had traveled from all over the country for the training sessions I was scheduled to facilitate. Focusing on their needs helped me stay in the moment, enabling me to function. I made a conscious choice to move my feelings to a *temporary* parking lot, confident that I would process everything when I felt safe. I didn't know Peggy Huddleston was also a psychotherapist!

The following Monday morning couldn't come fast enough. Sitting in my car outside her Boston office, I wondered how she might help me. I considered myself very resourceful, yet it seemed that the state of New Jersey had beaten me. The Adoption Agency was following outdated laws and I couldn't see a path forward. The clock was ticking; the cancer could progress at any time. Facing the possibility that I made the wrong decision by delaying was not an option. I said a quick prayer for clarity as I knocked on her office door.

Peggy Huddleston opened the door and greeted me warmly. I felt an instant connection. Her intense and compassionate blue eyes seemed to peer into my very soul, as she welcomed me inside. I made myself comfortable on the couch, as she asked me to share what brought me to her. I explained that I had read her book in anticipation of having surgery, and then the unexpected message I received about my mother. She invited me to take my time as I shared everything that had happened since the phone call seven months earlier outside the Yoga Center. Peggy Huddleston was the lifeline I hoped she would be. She asked insightful questions that helped me weave the seemingly unrelated threads from my physical, emotional and spiritual journeys together. Helpful insights emerged as we talked and I processed my thoughts out loud.

"I am stunned by the depth of the emotional release discovering she's gone. It's confirming that my search for her has always been about more than family medical information." In the safety of the session, I was able to release the heavy emotional protective shield I had carried for a very long time. A creative energy emerged along with a determination to write a *new* healing story.

Peggy Huddleston reassured me she had seen this type of breakthrough in many of her patients following a life-threatening medical diagnosis. The events can serve as a wake-up call. A call, if answered, allows a person to look at their whole life to see what needs healing. Not just the physical components. Setting in motion a process that offers continued introspection, and conscious awakening, when fully embraced. This explanation aligned with the work I was doing with the help of my integrative health care team. My healing journey had already revealed new ways to live in balance and the importance of dropping limiting beliefs. As the session was winding down, Peggy asked me if there was anything else I wanted to discuss.

"Yes. I am frustrated that I can't find a path forward to get my mother's cause of death from the Adoption Agency. The surgery is scheduled in two weeks. I'm leaning towards cancelling again."

She gently pointed out that my focus was on what I didn't have and what the agency wouldn't give me, versus what I was trying to attain. We discussed how energy flows in the direction of what we focus on, and our conversation reminded me of discussions with friends who were fans of the book *The Secret*. I knew a little about the "Law of Attraction" from what they had shared with me. Peggy's observation was right. Since the phone call from the Adoption Agency, all I could think about was their unwillingness to help, the archaic sealed adoption laws and the unfairness of the entire situation. It was clear I was inadvertently blocking the possibility of new ideas and potential creative solutions. She also recommended a book by Esther and Jerry Hicks, called *Ask and It Is Given, the* actual sources for the book *The Secret.*

Regarding the surgery, I asked Peggy Huddleston for help with the healing visualizations and deep relaxation techniques mapped out in her book. Her response resonated and I knew it was the right next step.

"Since I am not a doctor, I can only show you healing methods of relaxation and visualization if a gynecologist is overseeing your care who says it is safe for you to delay having a hysterectomy. I can give you the name of a gynecologist at Massachusetts General Hospital in Boston who I'd recommend." I was thrilled to have help finding a respected surgeon from a major teaching institution who supported an integrated approach.

I felt lighter as I walked from her office to my car. It was as if a huge weight had been lifted from my shoulders. Buoyed with a new sense of optimism and a plan, I sat in stillness and listened for clarity about the surgery. I committed to discussing it with my health care team as soon as possible, knowing I needed more time to integrate everything that had happened. One thing I knew for certain…adding the steps from Peggy Huddleston's book, including listening to the relaxation recording twice a day while visualizing specific healing milestones, was an essential new component for healing. Clinical research had demonstrated that feeling peaceful strengthens the immune system and creates the biochemistry that enhances healing. I began to visualize healthy cells lining my uterus, and healthy reports from upcoming imaging appointments. Additionally, I recognized the need to calm my nervous system outside of the times I was practicing yoga or listening to the relaxation recording. Reducing my eighty-hour travel filled work week, adding things that made me happy, eliminating people and things that did not support my highest good were the important changes I needed to implement. Immediately. Cancer became the catalyst for profound life changes.

A few days after my appointment, Dave and I headed down to New Jersey to visit his mother for Mother's Day. The seven-hour ride went by quickly as we listened to the audio book, *Ask and It Is Given,* by Jerry and Esther Hicks. The teachings were clearly explained and enhanced many of the books and courses we had attended over the years. My main takeaway was that I needed to get very clear on what I wanted to manifest regarding my birth mother's information. Next, I needed to release any resistance or doubt that it was possible. Once I understood the concepts, I could see how I was operating from a victim mindset. The book contained helpful techniques to shift focus and attention towards empowered feelings like optimism, love and appreciation. The technique that reduced my stress and anxiety the quickest was writing appreciation lists when I awoke in the morning and before I went to bed at night. I began to really *feel* how blessed my life was. Things that had happened in the past which I had labeled as "bad" were merely vehicles helping me arrive at the next level of understanding and awareness. Previously hidden layers of internal judgement fell away.

Self-care and prioritizing things that made me happy were the additional techniques offered. The book introduced the idea that instead of "wrestling your problems to the ground", change your state. Which in my case meant taking a walk, listening to music or dancing in Zumba. My logical mind liked to offer the opinion that these activities were a waste of time. I persevered, and discovered a shift. I was doing less efforting and more allowing. Inspirational ideas that resolved a challenging situation, or an ah-ha about a perplexing decision started to "come out of nowhere." I began to notice a connection between wrestling my problems to the ground, and my energy levels. Worry was sucking the vital energy right out of me. It was exhausting.

Additional books by Jerry and Esther Hicks introduced me to a curious concept about the benefits of knowing where you are on a "theoretical" emotional guidance system. Years of an eating disorder, augmented by workaholic perfectionism, had disconnected me from many of my feelings. I'm embarrassed to admit that for a time, I consulted the labels on the emotional scale in the book, to identify what I was actually feeling. For example, was I feeling hopeless or depressed? Angry or anxious? Admittedly, there were times when I thought the entire concept was crazy and a waste of my valuable time. However, there was no denying the impact my emotional state had on my physical healing. I was determined to give my body every opportunity to heal permanently, without surgery.

Regaining my original freedom became a game of identifying the emotion, courageously sitting with it, then allowing the feelings to simply pass through me. I became a witness, a detached observer to my thoughts. The process was liberating as insights were integrated and victimhood was left behind. The therapies Dr. Moore used, such as sound healing and acupuncture, continued to support the gentle release of buried emotions. I was healing from the inside out.

I came to understand the impact of avoiding or burying uncomfortable feelings. Opportunities to fully embrace life with excitement and anticipation were also dampened. Much like a radio tuned to a talk-show station is unable to play a top-40 channel, so too is selecting the worry station and expecting it to play happiness and appreciation. They reside at completely different frequencies.

While I was enjoying a quiet afternoon at the ocean, an idea came to me that would change my life. What if I applied Peggy Huddleston's specific healing methodology utilizing the deep relaxation recording and visualization techniques to find information about my birth mother's death? In addition to visualizing physically healing, I could add a specific end-result related to finding information about my birth mother. That evening, while listening to the relaxation recording before bed, I visualized my birth mother's full name and family location on a piece of paper. I saw myself driving with it carefully placed on the passenger seat of my car and under my pillow at night. I imagined what it would feel like. Just like the physical healing visualizations, I focused on seeing and feeling it happening in the present moment. *Ask and It is Given* suggests that the universe doesn't listen to what you say; it responds to how you feel. Which begged the question, *Did I really believe that after three decades of failed attempts and closed doors, I could use visualization technique to find her?*

From everything I had been learning – the case studies in *Prepare for Surgery, Heal Faster,* Dr. Northrup's work on the body-mind-spirit connection, and the *Law of Attraction* – I came to believe anything was possible. When doubts crept in, I imagined a reunion with my birth mother's family, sitting around the kitchen table, sharing stories, and looking through photo albums. The physical healing component consisted of envisioning a normal biopsy report and celebrating my eightieth birthday with friends and family. I saw and felt loved and appreciated, happy, healthy, and fully recovered without surgery. I visualized all these end results while listening to the deep relaxation recording, at least twice a day.

A few weeks later, as I laid my head on the pillow, I offered a heartfelt prayer of gratitude along with a request for help with the search for my mother's cause of death. In addition to the self-effort I was exercising, I had also come to a place of surrender and grace. I awoke the next morning with a clear directive: "Call the Adoption Agency and get your mother's death date. With the pieces you already have, you will find your answers."

11

THE ADOPTION DETECTIVE

*"The moon taught me: it's ok to go through phases.
The sun taught me: no matter how many times
you go down, keep rising!"*

I contacted the Adoption Agency later that morning, and apologized for my outburst of anger during the last call. Surely, they would understand my distress over realizing I would never meet the woman who brought me into this world. "Honoring and commemorating her passing each year would be a comfort," I explained to the social worker. "Would you please send me the date that she died?" Fortunately, I had the foresight to not divulge the information already in my possession about my birth mother. If they chose to give me her death date, I'd have an important new piece. Although I honestly had no idea what to do with it! I chose to put my trust in the guidance from the dream, and see where it led.

There were many guardian angels on my healing journey. One of the most helpful was my work colleague, Mary. She had given me Peggy's book as a gift, which proved a major gateway to dropping limiting beliefs and believing in conscious healing. Over lunch, I shared my dream and the call to the Adoption Agency for the death date. Because of a marketing research project she had worked on, she knew about something called the Social Security Index site. Every person that dies with a Social Security number is listed in an enormous data base. The trick is having two identifying pieces of information in order to locate the right person. Talking it through with Mary, I realized how much information I already possessed. I knew approximately how old my mother was when she gave birth, her first and middle names, and that at some point she lived in New Jersey, and then either Ohio or Kentucky, where she lived on a farm with seven children. The death date was an "identifying fact" essential to complete a search using the Social Security Index site. Mercifully, I didn't have to wait long. I was feeling significant pressure after canceling the surgery to discover her cause of death. Three days later, on May 23, 2010 at 10:00 am, I received an email from the Adoption Agency with an attached copy of my Mother's obituary notice. Of course, all identifying information was deleted, replaced by empty spaces. Only non-identifying information remained. I had seen this movie before, yet this time, there would be a new ending.

I called Dave from my speaker phone. I was going to need his calming presence. This was the moment I'd been envisioning the past few weeks. At the beginning of the obituary notice was her death date: September 19, 2009.

Oh my! She died just ten days after I received my cancer diagnosis. Is it possible she was guiding my healing journey and search for her from the other side?

The notice from the Funeral Home read:

_____passed away at midnight Saturday, September 19, 2009 at her home around midnight. Born

_____, survivors include _____(the blanks went on forever as there was a husband and seven adult children)

The funeral service will be held at 11:00 Thursday at the _____ Funeral home with Pastor John Thomas. Burial will immediately follow in _____Cemetery. Friends may call from 5 to 8 pm Wednesday at the funeral home. View this obituary and leave condolences at _____."

As I typed the Social Security web address into the search bar, my heart was pounding and every cell in my body alert with anticipation. My fingers struggled to type her first and middle name with no mistakes. I pressed enter and waited. About 40 names with some derivation of Mildred Lois appeared, along with multiple columns of information. The first column next to the names listed birth dates and the second column, death dates. I quickly found an exact match for the death date I had just received.

Would the associated birth date be the right year?

The birth date was November 26, 1938, placing her as seventeen when I was born. Incredibly, another match. Scrolling one more column to the left revealed a complete name: Mildred Lois Quigley.

Could this really be her?

I paused to look at the column headers and was relieved to discover I knew the remaining two pieces of requested information. Next, the first state where the Social Security card number was issued, and the state where the last check was mailed. Mildred Lois Quigley's row stated New Jersey for place of issue. Another match, as I knew she had lived in New Jersey when I was born.

If the next row contained either Ohio or Kentucky, I found my mother.

"It says Ohio" I screamed into the phone. "This has to be her!" I was greeted by enthusiastic cheering and clapping as Dave responded with an enthusiastic "Yes!"

I quickly took a picture capturing all her information, convinced my screen would freeze and I wouldn't be able to retrace my steps back. In order to confirm that this indeed was my birth mother, finding the exact obituary notice the Adoption Agency had sent was critical. Assuming the social worker wouldn't have spent much time on this request, I selected the first search option. After plugging in all the required information, I was one click away from getting what I had been seeking for decades. I took a deep breath and pressed enter. My heart skipped a beat as the computer screen went black. I prayed it was processing and not frozen. An obituary notice slowly began to appear on the screen. At a quick glance, this obituary notice looked like a match. Reading the information on my screen aloud to Dave so he could cross check the notice was the final verification step. Defying all odds, the obituary notice I was reading was an identical match with the one the agency had emailed that morning!

I pressed print screen, and began pacing the floor waiting an eternity for the printer to finish. After years of closed doors and sealed files, I had in my hand all the necessary information to find out the cause of her death. And more. Her husband's name and address, as well as all the adult children. From the town names, I could tell everyone but the youngest brother lived close to the farmstead. More research would be needed to determine if Mildred's husband was my father. Incredibly, I went from being an adopted only child to being the oldest of eight. I contacted my nephew Adam, who is a computer genius, and asked him to do as much research as he possibly could. I needed data before I made any overtures towards the family.

Incredibly, a mere four weeks after learning my mother had died, I was in possession of my birth mother's full name. Tears of joy streaked my face as I made my way to the office of a dear friend and colleague to share the news. She had survived her own cancer diagnosis and was very invested in my progress. We talked about the deep relaxation and visualization process I learned from the book *Prepare for Surgery, Heal Faster,* as well as Peggy Huddleston's workshop and my health care teams' integrated approach. I had no doubt my intuition had been greatly enhanced. In just four weeks of hearing the news about my mother, I had the information necessary to assemble ALL the missing pieces. I had no doubt that divine intervention played a key role. My prayer for guidance had been answered the very next morning. As I walked to my car at the end of the day, I wondered:

Was it an accident that my diagnosis came just weeks before my mother left this earth plane?

Had she been the messenger delivering clues in my dreams?

My mother had just given me the one thing she wasn't able to give me when she was alive…her identity.

I drove around for weeks with one copy of the obituary notice printout placed on the passenger seat of my car, another copy in the safety deposit box with other irreplaceable items, and the third gently placed under my pillow. It helped me feel physically connected to my birth mother.

The adoption detective work was far from over. Important questions about her cause of death, the best way to approach my new family, the identity of my birth father and his medical background all demanded answers. The most immediate question was finding the cause of her death. It was a surprisingly easy and fast process. There was a line in the online application requesting her death certificate that gave me pause. It asked for the "connection to the deceased?"

Typing in the word "daughter" took me a moment to process. *Was this okay? Can I really claim this?* The death certificate took just a few days to arrive. Scanning the document, I breathed a sigh of relief. "The cause of death was emphysema from a lifetime of smoking." She did not die from breast, ovarian or uterine cancer.

There was a lot to consider regarding my next move. I couldn't show up on family members' doorsteps, asking questions like in a Hallmark Movie. This was a real family with memories about their wife and mother. If I was a secret that no one in the family knew, approaching them the right way was important. Online research found some published technical papers from the oldest brother. Other than that, not much surfaced. Knowing the cause of her death reinforced that I had time to continue my non-surgical healing journey. During my next appointment with Dr. Moore I wondered aloud, "How did finding my birth mother's identity impact my healing journey?" As well as, "Would the release of buried emotions accelerate my physical healing?" It had certainly helped shift my emotional and mental states. We agreed to follow the treatment plan and monitor my physical status with Western imaging technology. I continued listening to Peggy Huddleston's relaxation recording twice a day, creating new end results for the midsummer and September progress checks. I shared the latest entry in my journal with Dr. Moore.

"It was unimaginable just a month ago, that I would have the necessary information to meet my birth family. Yet, it happened. I believe I can now fully embrace the idea that it is possible for my body to heal without surgical intervention. This time, with full conviction and no reservations."

Two months later I felt ready to reach out to my mother's family. Significant research had been completed and everyone at work was eager to offer their suggestions, opinions and counter-options regarding the best approach. There were many votes for sending a letter to the oldest son asking for family medical information. This idea was also met with resistance.

"No way. He might not appreciate that he is no longer the oldest, and accidently lose your letter."

Others suggested the oldest daughter. As a woman, she would have compassion and feelings about the situation.

"Bad idea. As the oldest daughter, she was likely the closest to her mother."

What to do? I was feeling torn between the youngest brother and the oldest sister.

Someone suggested a pendulum test over all the names. I was getting used to unconventional methods, so why not. Not surprising, the pendulum hovered between the exact siblings I had felt pulled towards. I chose the youngest brother. He was in his late 30s at the time, and the only one to move out of state. Maybe he would be the least threatened and the most likely to help? I was driving myself crazy with all the possibilities. In the end, I found there is no substitute for following intuition with what felt right in my body. After a particularly deep sound-healing session, the next step appeared clearly. I would write a letter and mail it to *all* the siblings at the same time. Let them decide if they wanted to tell their father. As Dr. Moore and I left her office, we looked up and saw hundreds of dragonflies circling above us. I already had a connection with the dragonfly totem from my mother's passing. From the Native tradition, the dragonfly as spirit animal carries the wisdom of transformation and adaptability. I took them as a sign of confirmation and blessing.

I put myself in my family's shoes as I sat at my desk to write the letter. How would they feel hearing that their mother had another daughter? What words could I use to minimize the impact of the news? I was interested in the extended family medical history, sisters, aunts, grandmothers, and of course something that I could now willingly admit… more information about my mother. I said a prayer, put on a cd with sacred mantras and wrote from my heart.

"There is no way to start a letter like this. And the only reason I am writing to each of you, is I am in need of medical information. Your mother was also my mother. Maybe this is not a surprise? Your mother had me when she was seventeen, while living in New Jersey. I was placed for adoption, and grew up about 45 minutes north of where she lived. I have been dealing with a cancer diagnosis and an upcoming surgery. I am not seeking anything from you, except health information. I am hoping you can find it in your heart to reach out to me."

Wanting to reassure them I wasn't a crazy person, I sent pictures of Dave and I and the kitties. I wanted to depict a "normal" family, and hoped they would forgive me for dropping this on them. Afterall, they had lost their mom just nine months earlier. I placed the seven letters on my meditation altar and waited for the auspicious full moon coming in a couple of weeks. According to ancient traditions, the July full moon is a time to honor your past and present teachers, including the divine source that resides inside each of us. This seemed like the perfect time. Dave and I blessed each letter with the heartfelt intention that my request would be heard. The answer came just three days later. A new journey of possibility was about to start.

12
BELONGING

*"In the silence inside we find peace. We find ourselves.
Our whole selves. PEACE is a place we never left."*

—Lee Harris

The next medical milestone for monitoring my progress was a six-month imaging appointment. My plan was to work half a day and then drive to the Imaging Center in Boston. I awoke with an overwhelming feeling to stay home, and use a personal day. A benefit of my mind-body-spirit integrated approach was enhanced intuition, as I was learning to tune in more. The message was particularly clear; sit for meditation. I selected the sacred chant, Om Namah Shivaya, which invokes and honors the divine consciousness within. The melody put me into a state of deep relaxation, and worry about my upcoming imaging appointment began to ease and release. Time disappeared, and my mind became quiet. On this day, it seemed "my future self" knew something significant was about to happen and wanted me grounded and prepared. While in the shower, I missed a phone call and voice mail from an unfamiliar number. *Was it possible one of my siblings had received the letter already?* The letters had just been mailed two days earlier, and it was only noontime on Wednesday.

My heart pounding in anticipation, I grabbed my journal and prepared myself to listen to the message.

"Chris, this is Steve." *I knew it would be the youngest brother.*

"Got your letter today. And it's come as a complete surprise to me, my siblings, *and* my dad."

Oh my, my mother's husband already knows?

Steve took a long pause. *Okay, this is it. Now he's going to blast me for lying and invading their lives.*

"Soooo ... call me back. You have my number."

I was stunned. That's it? He was actually offering to help?

Unable to contain my relief, tears overflowed and I called Dave. His response surprising, "It feels like this is the first time you have truly exhaled!"

"So true. I've waited my entire life for this moment."

Recognizing the importance of what was about to happen I pulled myself together, retrieved my favorite pen, dated a new page in my journal and called my brother.

"This is Chris. I can't believe my letter came so quickly. I'm really grateful you called me." The words just poured out, explaining my search efforts since turning 18. He asked me how he could help. I laughed, "Well, I have a lot of questions."

"What did they call Mom? I had seen Mildred and Lois in my research."

Steve explained her Ohio friends and family called her Millie. The Kentucky family called her by her middle name, Lois.

"What was she like?"

Steve's response spoke volumes for how he revered his mother. He described her as beautiful, with long hair below her waist, usually worn braided and coiled on top of her head. She was generous and kind, always rescuing animals and helping neighbors in need.

"What's our nationality?"

Steve was positive about being Irish with a strong possibility that we were also Native American. He wasn't sure which tribe. He had heard maybe Blackfeet.

If it proved true, it would explain my appreciation and concern for Indigenous cultures. In junior high, a movie called *Little Big Man* with Dustin Hoffman had moved me to tears and outrage. This was my first exposure to the atrocities the original inhabitants of North America experienced. I followed up with letters to the United States government, inquiring about their current treatment. My adopted family was totally baffled, and didn't understood my interest. When I was old enough to travel, I fell in love with the Southwest and Montana. Which was interesting, as the land in Glacier National Park was the original home of the Blackfeet. Over time, our Native collection of pottery, paintings, and rugs from the various Indigenous Tribes turned the interior of our Maine seacoast home into a curiosity. Steve's revelation reminded me of the nature vs nurture debate. *Was my interest in Indigenous Cultures part of my genetic makeup and in my DNA?* One of my favorite hiking pictures was taken in Glacier National Park. My chestnut brown hair was parted in the middle, with two long braids framing my face. With a purple bandana around my forehead, my reddish-brown tan, dark eyes, and high cheekbones, I always thought I looked like a Native American woman. Despite my family's insistence that I was Irish.

"That explains a lot," I said to Steve, as new pieces came together.

"Did she really die from emphysema?"

Steve confirmed that this was accurate. She had started smoking as a young teenager. Steve shared she had been ill for the past ten years, and her death had been a slow, painful process to experience. There was little he could do to help as her illness progressed.

"Did anyone in the family have cancer?"

His response opened a door into family dynamics. "Our grandmother Agnes died from "old age and meanness.""

I quickly learned the siblings were not fond of their grandmother yet worshipped her husband, Grandad Quigley. There were no aunts or sisters who had cancer. Even though this was only half of my medical history, it was still reassuring.

"How did your dad respond when he found out about the letters?"

"You know, that's a very interesting question. I thought he would freak out. He is a red neck from rural Ohio, you know." Steve repeated Fred's exact words: "Interesting. Why don't you give her a call and see what's she's like?" Steve explained this was a highly unusual response, and not what he expected.

He asked me if I wanted pictures. I chuckled and explained, "For my entire life I wondered if I resembled anyone else on the planet. I also have some physical features that are odd and wondered where they had come from. I've got two short and stumpy thumbs that look like there's a digit missing." I thoroughly enjoyed Steve's laugh as I continued, "I didn't realize how weird they were until I was in junior high. A bunch of us went bowling, and I couldn't fit my thumb into a youth bowling ball. I had to pick up an adult ball. You can imagine how well that went."

Steve commiserated with my predicament, yet knew nothing about the family's thumbs. However, we did share a lazy right eye. He promised to send pictures of Mom from his wedding, just two years earlier. "Thank you. This is a gift beyond my wildest dreams."

He added some of the other siblings would be in touch soon, and offered insights into their various personalities. Steve's descriptions contained a protective quality, a completely foreign concept for me growing up as an only child.

Minutes after saying goodbye, Steve sent my first photo of my mother from his cell phone. I enlarged it as much as possible, to make out all the details and look for resemblances. Millie was standing between Steve and her husband, Fred. She was petite and visibly ill with an oxygen cannula in her nostrils to help her breathe. Her face was gaunt, with a prominent forehead, thin lips, and a kind smile. It was hard for me to see any resemblance from this photo. I did see common features with Steve, even with our eighteen-year age difference; same cheekbones, square jaw, and deep-set eyes. There are no adequate words that convey what I felt looking into the faces of my biological family for the first time. It was as if I were seeing myself for the first time. I detected Native ancestry in my mother's gaunt face. I thought about the deep connection I feel when I'm out in nature. It was not something I learned from my adopted family. Steve's revelation of possible Blackfeet meant a lot to me. While backpacking in Glacier, I learned a lot about their beliefs and honoring the divine spirit in all things. The tribes that managed to survive unspeakable genocide remember the language and the conversation of how the earth and the sky speak to us.

First picture

After Steve's call, there were interesting ways his new information influenced my work life. One curious experience happened while I was preparing for a department budget presentation. Not only was I presenting to the senior executive team in the board room, I was asking for a budget increase. I had a familiar feeling of anxiety and butterflies in my stomach as I grabbed my folder and left my office. On the way to the board room, I stopped at the restroom for a final opportunity to organize my thoughts and breathe. Looking in the mirror, a feeling of confidence and determination arose as I heard the words, "You come from a strong and powerful people who survived against great odds. Surely, you can handle a budget meeting." I laughed out loud and continued to the board room, shoulders set and head held high. It was the first time I drew on my ancestral lineage for support. And they didn't let me down. I left the board room with our department budget increase secured.

Following the call with Steve, I still had to drive to Boston for my imaging appointment. I called Dave on the drive into the city, bursting to share the details. There was much to process, and I wondered aloud about the curious timing of Steve's call.

"No one could orchestrate this timing. The day I receive answers to lifelong questions just happens to coincide with an important imaging progress evaluation?"

"The synchronicity is hard to dismiss and raises some interesting questions," Dave responded.

"So true. I made a promise and closed the door on continuing to search for Mom when the social worker told me I was a secret not to be revealed. It took a serious diagnosis with a surgical intervention to break my promise and re-ignite my search.

"Something is shifting in my perception about the possibility of a bigger purpose regarding my cancer diagnosis. I've been fixating on asking, 'Why is this happening to me and how can I fix it and get back to my life?'

"Do I sound totally crazy?"

As Dave encouraged me to continue, I silently thanked God for giving me such a supportive partner.

"A new question is emerging, 'How is what's happening helping me evolve and expand beyond my limiting beliefs about what's possible?'"

"Whatever it is, it feels like a major breakthrough," Dave offered.

"Yes. It's as if I'm being guided to step firmly onto a new path that involves reclaiming my inherent worthiness."

And finally, *the* question found its voice. I asked in amazement at the implication, "If my emotional body is dropping old beliefs and healing buried wounds, what's stopping my physical body from healing completely... without surgery? After all, the point of an integrated healing approach is considering the interconnectedness between body-mind-spirit, right?" Dave reminded me of his physical healing experience with arthritis and how he let go of past wrongs and stopped being his own harsh critic. He became less rigid and more flexible in his approach to life. Living in the moment became a natural way of being for him.

"The cancer diagnosis was not only the catalyst for my search, it also forced me to push the giant *pause* button on my life. A pause that created space for stillness and enhanced intuition. Staying home to meditate this morning is a perfect example. My future self knew it was going to be a big day, and it gave me the chance to tap into resources that would support me a few hours later.

"Dave, this may sound utterly mad, but here goes. Is there any need for the cancer part of this journey to continue? Or has it served its purpose? I think a new door just opened into an unseen realm beyond anything I can explain with my scientific mind. I'm going to go way out on a limb here," I teased, preparing him for the proclamation I was about to make.

"I believe the imaging results later this afternoon will be normal. I'll know soon. I'm about to pull into the parking garage."

"So be it," was his perfect response.

Following the ultrasound exam, the radiologist came in to review my results. Incredibly, there were no signs of any abnormalities. She was very surprised and reviewed the results multiple times with a colleague. I didn't bother to explain that for months I visualized healthy cells and focused on my body's innate ability to heal itself. She wouldn't have believed me. Later that evening, my scientific mind reminded me that another biopsy should be done to confirm that only healthy cells remained. The additional data would support what I felt intuitively.

In the meantime, I was looking forward to conversations with additional siblings, wondering who would call next. It would be Sis, the oldest sister in the original family configuration. She was generous with more family information and had anticipated my desire for more pictures, and a package was on its way already. I liked her efficiency immediately. We laughed about the "nature vs nurture" revelations regarding our likes and dislikes. We shared peculiar things like cherry Coke and Bavarian hard pretzels as treats, our dislike of beer and coffee, and our shared lab backgrounds. And best of all, the answer to the stumpy thumb origin. Sis and Mom were proud owners of one stumpy, short thumb on each hand, confirming them as a maternal trait. Sis promised to stay in touch. Feeling we were kindred spirits, I looked forward to meeting her in person.

The next communication from Ohio would be the most unexpected and most profound. It happened on a Saturday morning while I was driving home from yoga. I recognized the number now as an Ohio area code, but it wasn't Sis or Steve. An older male voice with a Midwest, nasal accent introduced himself.

"Chris, this is Fred. Millie's husband."

Seriously? I never expected to hear from him, assuming he was getting the information he wanted from the kids as they contacted me. I was overjoyed to talk directly with him. With my mother's passing, he was the closest person to her. Fred started our conversation with, "Imagine my surprise…"

Of course, he was surprised to hear about the letters from Steve.

"…when I heard from Millie that she had a daughter in 1956, when she was 17."

It was my turn to be surprised. *Someone actually knew about me beyond my mother and grandmother.*

"You were born two years before I met your mother. Your grandmother, Agnes, swore Millie to secrecy. She reminded her as a young adult that no one would want her if they knew she had a baby. Your mother kept her secret completely to herself until 1974, after her father was killed in an explosion on the Delaware River."

I was barely able to contain myself. I was about to find out what my mom said about me. I found it curious that Steve and Sis hadn't mentioned any of this. Wanting to not miss anything Fred said, I found a safe place to pull off the road.

"Fred, I am so blown away that you called. I started searching for Mom when I turned eighteen. Every few years I contacted the Adoption Agency to see if they had any updated information about Mom. I stayed optimistic that the laws in New Jersey would someday be changed, and then around 1993, I hit an unexpected block. A new social worker started working on finding Mom, picking up where the last search had left off with the last phone number on file. She spoke with someone who said they were speaking on Mom's behalf. The woman relayed that 'No one in the family knew about me, and if anyone found out, it would destroy the family.' The worst part is the woman refused any contact from me; not even pictures with a letter. I was devastated."

Fred grumbled the name, "Agnes."

"Damn her," he continued. "Your grandmother was constantly meddling and trying to control your mother." He went on to explain that he and Mom married in 1958. They moved from New Jersey to Ohio, where Fred's family lived, initially living in a small house in the town of Lisbon. Their family grew rapidly and they moved out to a farm, about 20 minutes out of town so the children had space, and where they could have animals.

"Honey, the woman that took the call from the social worker was your grandmother Agnes, not your mother. Agnes stayed in the Lisbon house, after we moved out to the farm. I am positive your grandmother never told your mother about that phone call. Your mother wanted to find you. We talked about what information she had and how we could find you. Back then there was no Internet, and the only thing she knew about you was that your adopted parents were Catholic and lived somewhere in New Jersey. The more we talked, the more we realized that finding you would be impossible with the little information we had. Plus, she had no way of knowing if you knew you were adopted. We discussed that even if we could find you, how could we just show up?"

I chuckled, "I can definitely relate to that question. I waited months before I sent the letters. I assumed it would be a shock so it took some time to find the best way to approach everyone."

I realized my cheeks were wet with tears as the information that someone knew I existed overwhelmed me. I had always wished that my mother hadn't blocked me out of her memory, and that she wanted to find me. Even more important was the discovery that the "woman speaking on my mother's behalf" was NOT. The past-life regression therapy session months earlier had been accurate. Not only had the session exposed that my grandmother was the one blocking me, it also confirmed that Millie wanted to be found! Damn Agnes for sure. My grandmother robbed me of the chance to meet my mother when she was young and healthy. I calculated she would have been about fifty years old at that point.

"Fred, is Grandmother Agnes still alive? If so, I'm not sure I could be in the same room with her."

"No, honey. She died a few years ago from complications from smoking."

With time and reflection, I was able to release my resentment toward my grandmother. I would have struggled taking care of the elders in my adopted family while being involved with my new birth family. My relationship with my aunts and uncles had only deepened after my adopted parents had died, and I didn't think they would understand my desire to find my birth family. I would have done anything for them and never wanted them to think "they weren't enough" for me. Whatever the reason, a reunion with my birth mother was not meant to be, and I missed finding her by eight months. I asked Fred why she waited so long to tell him about me.

"I was best friends with your grandfather. While captaining a barge on the Delaware River that separates Pennsylvania from New Jersey, there was an explosion and fire. He saved many of his crew, but was later found dead trapped under a dock. Your mother waited to tell me about you until grandad was gone. She didn't want to give me the burden of keeping such a big secret."

"You mean her own father never knew I was born?" I asked dumbfounded.

"Your Grandad never knew your mother was pregnant. He spent long periods of time out at sea. She became pregnant with you while he was on a long deployment. Agnes arranged your adoption while he was gone. No one in the family knew about you except your mother and grandmother, then me, years later. And your grandmother never knew that I knew about you. You were a secret your mother and I shared together.

"And yet another secret Mom had to keep. Only this time, it was from her mother," I added. *How completely exhausting.* I had trouble keeping a secret about buying new shoes! One could only imagine the pain she must have felt keeping the birth and adoption of her daughter a secret from her own father.

Fred continued with additional details, "Before your mother told me about you, I always thought something was wrong with her, but I couldn't figure out what it was. The whole family would be together celebrating Christmas or a birthday, and when I looked over at her, she had a sad, distant look on her face. In the beginning, I asked what was wrong. She always said nothing, and over time I stopped asking. Her moods put a strain on our marriage. It was as if she built a wall around herself to keep me out."

Of course, they would have struggled. The pressure to keep something so personal from the person closest to you must have been painful. It made me think about what young mothers in similar situations experienced. The trauma wasn't just isolated at the point when they had to leave their babies in the hospital. The trauma would live silently in them forever. If they had other children, everyone around them would congratulate them on their "first" baby. The mothers would know this was not their first, and their grief or pain would be re-triggered with each new child born. No wonder my mother had built a protective wall around herself. There was a lot of pain to try to keep out. Fred's next comment echoed my thoughts.

"It was not surprising that there were times your mother looked distant and detached. After I found out about you, I felt bad that she endured her pain in silence for so many years."

I really liked this man who married my mother. He was considerate and thoughtful. I shared with Fred that my birthday was always a time of quiet contemplation.

Wondering where she was, what was her life was like, and did she think about me.

"Now you know that she *was* thinking of you and *not* just on your birthday." It seemed mother and daughter shared an invisible thread connecting us beyond time and distance. Incredibly, Fred had more to share.

"When Steve called to tell me about your letter, I had a problem. At the time your mother told me about you, we decided not to share her secret with the children. When Steve asked me what to do about your letter, I was stuck. I had made a promise to your mother and your letter changed things. I asked Steve to call you and see what you were like. I needed more time. I went down to the cemetery to talk with Millie. I told her about your letter and that you needed our help. I asked her permission to tell the children. I'm not exaggerating one bit when I tell you this. I felt her hand on my shoulder, as she whispered 'yes.' I decided to tell all of them after Steve and Sis talked with you. They were curious but nobody freaked out," he added.

I thanked him for all the information, struggling with how to ask the next question.

"Fred, who was my birth dad? Did mom tell you?"

I learned a little about Fred's humor as he answered my question.

"Chrissy, it was hard enough finding out I wasn't her first. I didn't ask any questions."

"Fair enough," I chuckled, as my heart sank a little. I was hoping for a complete picture of my paternal medical history and ancestry. More detective work would be needed. Another question came to mind, and I hoped it wasn't pushing him too much.

"Fred, do you think it would be okay if I came to Ohio on the anniversary of mom's passing? I could meet everyone and visit her gravesite."

He barely paused, before saying, "Of course, you can come." I asked Fred to check with all the kids to make sure it was okay. This would be the first anniversary of their mother's passing, and my presence would change the family dynamics a lot. I thanked him from the bottom of my heart. Questions I had carried forever were finally answered. The call with Fred happened in August of 2010, eleven months after my diagnosis, and almost a year after my mother's death. I set a new intention to find my birth father by the end of the year, December, 2010. Something told me the answer was in my mother's house and my sisters would help me find it.

13

HEARTS UNITED

"We are caught in an inescapable network of mutuality; tied in a single garment of destiny. Whatever affects one directly, affects all indirectly."

—Dr. Martin Luther King, Jr.

My second sister, Len, called a few days later while Dave and I were on our way to one of our favorite places, Acadia National Park in Bar Harbor, Maine. I was looking forward to time off to rest, renew and reflect on the miraculous developments that had occurred over the past 11 months. I couldn't wait to lie on the pink granite boulders along the ocean shoreline and hike the pine trails of Acadia. This year had special significance, with so much to acknowledge and appreciate. Len called to tell me that everyone was fine with my visit on the one-year anniversary of mom's passing. Our first phone call lasted over two hours, as Dave drove through picturesque harbors and along the jagged coastline. Len also lived on a farm with her husband, children and many rescue animals. She apparently took after mom with her love of animals and caring for the ones no one wanted. Her laugh was robust, her words encouraging about my visit, and I really looked forward to meeting her in a few weeks. It was hard to believe that after a lifetime of searching, in just a few weeks I would be at my mother's house, meeting my birth family and honoring her gravesite.

Finding the perfect gift for her was important. The gift appeared while Dave and I were crossing from the main island of Bar Harbor onto Sand Bar Island. Left by the receding tide was a perfectly shaped heart stone. I found out from my sister Len that Mom loved the ocean and was an accomplished swimmer. I too have an inexplicable pull towards the ocean and was on the swim team. Len explained that Mom and our grandmother frequented Wildwood, a popular beach on the Atlantic Ocean an hour south from my home. Wildwood happened to be my adopted parents' favorite place to take me. It raised the possibility that my birth mother and I were on that beach at the same time. Imagining this Hallmark moment brought me closer to her. A heart stone from the Atlantic Ocean was the perfect gift to bring to honor my mother's memory.

While waiting to board the plane to Pittsburgh for the trip home to meet my family, I thought my heart was going to leap out of my chest. When Fred had called in August, he had mentioned mom was a "hillbilly" from Kentucky. I didn't really know what that meant. I had grown up on the East Coast, near a big city. Would we find common ground beyond the obvious? And finally, there would be an answer to the question Dave and I had debated for years: Whose version of the farm was correct, mine or Dave's?

When the social worker told me my birth mother lived on a farm somewhere on the border of Ohio or Kentucky,

Dave and I envisioned very different images of what the farm might look like. Dave saw a horse farm in Kentucky. I was certain it was a very lived-in farmhouse that had seen better days. In my mind's eye, there were chickens, an old tractor in the yard, and a porch with a couch. It wasn't long before we discovered whose version was accurate. The drive from the airport to meet my two sisters took us through three states, along winding country roads. We had arranged to meet them in the parking lot of a hotel just outside the closest town to the farm. As they got out of their cars, I recognized them immediately from the photos Sis had sent. Pictures from when we were children showed many physical characteristics; as adults, not as much. What we did share were hugs and a tear-filled reunion. Somehow the moment was both awkward and familiar. Before getting back into our cars to follow them to the farm, Sis grabbed my arm and offered a warning. *Oh no. Here comes some unexpected bombshell about the family.* Years earlier, on Mom's birthday, Steve, the youngest brother, had given Mom a wolf/dog pup named Kitona. She was now full grown, and with Mom gone, she had become very protective of Fred.

"Okay," I asked, "is there a protocol for how one greets a wolf dog?" They both laughed as I shared the headline that had popped into my mind:

"Woman from Maine is finally reunited with her birth family, after decades of searching, only to be mauled by the family dog!"

It turned out there was a recommended approach. Sis advised us not to make any sudden moves toward Fred, giving her time to get our scent.

Kitona, guardian and protector

Sounded straightforward, until we drove up the long dirt road leading to the farmhouse. My excitement intensified and I wasn't sure moving slowly toward Fred was an option. I was just a few steps away from hugging the person closest to the woman who gave me life.

The farm house came into view, and my version of my mother's house had been accurate. The house hadn't been painted in a very long time, with no paint left to even peel off. There was a front porch with a couch, and since it had been a working farm, there were tractors in the yard. No farm animals now, but there had been. The land was beautiful, with a large grassy hill beyond the house, surrounded by large trees splendid in their fall colors. We parked the car on the grass, and I could see Kitona on the porch sitting by Fred's side. I got out of the car, my heart pounding, as I walked as fast as I could without running. When I finally reached Fred, it was *the embrace* I had imagined. We both cried, and held onto each other for a long time. Fred reminded me of my Uncle Gus, with his khaki pants and flannel shirt. He was thin, his face weathered from years of working outside.

Like the first picture I had seen of my mother, Fred was connected to an oxygen tank. He was another casualty of the tobacco industry's marketing to young teens. He suffered from emphysema, and still smoked. Fred acknowledged he was dying; might as well enjoy whatever time he had left.

Surprising me with his openness Fred said, "I am lost every day without her. She was my best friend. I have no interest in 'sticking around' without her."

Fred formally introduced us to Kitona. She was a beautiful and well-fed adult wolf dog. Her intense yellow eyes seemed to peer right into my soul.

Chris, Fred and Sis September 2010

Introductions were made to the brothers and their wives. Of all the siblings, Steve and I seemed to have the most similarities in bone structure. Fred commented that I had thin lips, just like Mom's, and our laughs were similar. The sisters thought I moved like her, as well. Steve was excited to take us out on the trails behind the house on my first four-wheeled adventure. When we returned, they gifted me a fun T-shirt that I proudly put on.

Sis, Chris and Len

I took in my surroundings. From the couch in the living room, I noticed large pieces of plaster missing from the ceiling and walls, and the only light came from a bulb on the end of a wire hanging down from the center of the ceiling. Years of smoking stained the walls and ceiling. While I was taking it all in, Kitona came over to the couch and laid her head on my leg. Fred commented on how unusual that behavior was for her. She typically took a long time to warm up to "strangers." It's one of my favorite memories from the visit. She knew that I was *not* a stranger. It was a surreal experience as I vacillated between observer of what was happening, and experiencer. The surroundings were unfamiliar, yet instead of feeling strange I felt a surprising ease being with people I had never met before. *Was it was my mother's loving intention and presence radiating from Kitona that was contributing to the comfortable energy I was feeling?*

Cousins and additional siblings arrived, and the atmosphere shifted from welcoming to curious. They wanted all the details about who I was and how I found them. I was surprised at the level of acceptance they offered, and especially grateful for my mother's decision to tell Fred about me. She had prepared the path as best she could for the possibility of this day. Family stories were shared and a picture emerged of what life was like on the farm. Years without electricity and running water had made for challenging times. Fred had worked various jobs, including in the coal mines, which explained his health challenges at the young age of 73. I found my mind wandering to a very different scenario. If my grandmother had made a different decision in 1956 instead of growing up in a suburban town in New Jersey with access to Philadelphia and New York, I would have been the oldest of eight, on a farm in rural Ohio. Some in the family described Millie and Fred as "old school" when it came to social norms that I grew up taking for granted. For example, they did not support their oldest daughter, Sis, going to college. She would not be denied. Sis worked multiple jobs to pay for college and graduated with a degree in social work. I resonated with both sisters' independent spirits, as we shared experiences, hopes and dreams.

Diving into a wonderful buffet of food as everyone congregated around the kitchen table, I was struck with the contrast between the family gatherings I was used to, and what was happening in the kitchen of the farmhouse. When the family that raised me was fully assembled, there would be seven of us! Here, we were bursting at the seams, with people throughout the house and yard. I was anxious to hear more about the family. Universally, the spouses described Millie as kind, and always willing to help others less fortunate. She especially loved ducks, even bringing them into a wading pool in the basement during the winter. Interestingly, a few months later, Dave and I found Mom's childhood home in New Jersey. She lived near a large lake in the center of town filled with birds and ducks. We wondered if the ducks on the farm in Ohio reminded her of a simpler time? Everyone agreed that Mom was very pretty, her long brown hair turning silver as she aged. Her pictures before she became ill reminded me of the Native American grandmothers I had met, with her long braids coiled atop her head.

After dinner, we heard more about the grandparents. Grandad seemed universally loved, his wife Agnes, not so much. My grandmother was described as protective and overbearing. She had several sisters, and they thought Aunt Hazel was still alive, living near the original homestead in Kentucky. I made a mental note to talk with Sis about a road trip. Millie's parents moved the family from Kentucky to South Jersey when she was a young girl. They wanted her to have more opportunities than the hard life on the farm. Grandad worked on ships and barges traveling the world, often returning with gifts from the ports he visited. Depending on who was telling the story, there were multiple versions of Grandmother Agnes' life raising Millie in their small bungalow near the Delaware River tributaries. On one hand, she was a struggling mother, raising her only daughter mostly alone. In the other version, she was a young woman, often seen in nice clothes, fur coat and jewelry. Some suggested parties and infidelity when her husband was out at sea. Not up for dispute was Grandmother's protective and stifling nature when it came to her daughter.

I was curious about Mom's time in New Jersey. Apparently, life with her mother had been challenging, and Millie looked forward to visiting the Kentucky homestead each summer. She had nine cousins to play with, and two of them, Janet and Ruth Ann, were mentioned as "best friends" to Mom. I made a mental note to see if we could find them. Perhaps

Mom had confided in them secretly, against her mother's wishes. And maybe they knew who my birth father was. Mom's photo albums confirmed her love for the farm and she was usually seen with the goats, sheep, or chickens.

Millie enjoying the Kentucky farm chores

Two years after I was born, at the age of nineteen, Millie met Fred, who was stationed at a nearby Army base in Delaware. They met at a friend's wedding and following a short courtship, they married. When Millie became pregnant with their first son, they decided to leave the busyness of South Jersey and moved to Ohio, to be closer to Fred's parents. And as far away as possible from Agnes, Fred added.

I had heard about the tragic death of Grandad during my first phone call with Fred. There was considerable pride around the kitchen table, as the family remembered him as a hero, pulling many men to safety from the burning wreckage. Tragically, Grandad drowned in the river he had loved. Agnes rejoined Fred and Millie in Ohio after Grandad's death, and that's where my story intersected Fred's. I recounted the call with the social worker who called the last number they had had on file for Mom. I explained the social worker connected with a woman who said "she was speaking on Mom's behalf." She communicated that I was a secret and they would not accept any communication from me or the social worker in the future. This generated the same response Fred had given me over the phone.

"Damn Agnes." Everyone jumped as one of the brothers banged his fist on the table.

Sis said what everyone was thinking. "We could have met sooner. You would have had time with Mom when she was healthy." There was a long pause as everyone took that in. Overwhelmed with emotion as images arose of "what might have been," I could no longer hold back the tears.

Fred jumped back into telling his part of the story. The adult children and their spouses were very curious about who knew what and when. Fred shared that he didn't find out until Grandad died, about twenty years after they had been married. He and Millie made a conscious decision not to tell anyone about me. No one spoke as the realization of the burden Millie carried settled in. One of the sisters-in-law commented that Mom often suffered from severe headaches and depression at various times in her life. I thought about the books I had been reading about the mind-body-spirit connections. She likely buried emotions like shame, anger, sadness and grief just to survive. *How interesting that her illness impacted her ability to breathe and speak and was located in the heart region?* My thoughts were interrupted when one of my brothers pointed to a rifle in the corner of the living room, a smile spreading across his face lightening the mood. "Damn good thing Mom told Dad about you. Dad's a proud redneck and outsiders telling stories about family aren't welcome here." I whispered another prayer of gratitude for Mom's foresight.

Looking at Millie and Fred's wedding pictures, I was reminded of a young Audrey Hepburn and Frank Sinatra. They were a beautiful couple. I asked Fred in private if there was any significance to the date he and Millie were married. They had been married June 10, 1958, two years after my birth. He never knew why she had chosen that date, and she never offered an explanation. Recalling her insistence on that date, I knew intuitively that their June wedding date had something to do with me. I made another mental note to discuss it with my two sisters. They were becoming welcome additional research partners.

Fred and Millie June 10, 1958

The following morning, a small group of us headed to the cemetery. The air was perfectly still as we drove up the lane of the small country cemetery behind the church. The edge of the cemetery was ringed by a beautiful stand of trees already changing color. Fred guided me to Mom's gravesite, and I gently placed the heart stone against her headstone.

On the back of the stone, I had written, "Our hearts, united again. Love always, your daughter." The wind began to swirl around us, rising out of nowhere. As fast as it rose, it disappeared. Fred, Sis, Dave, and I took it as a sign from Mom that the gift had been received with love.

Heart stone on mom's gravesite

We headed to Len's house to meet her family and visit her rescued farm animals. She had a horse saddled up and ready for me. I was proudly wearing my new T-shirt, and completely at peace as we rode across the open fields. We had a tearful good-bye later that afternoon, and back at the farm house, I left with a promise to come back for Thanksgiving, and Mom's November birthday. The day after we returned home, I received a call from Fred. He told me that after I left the farm house, Kitona visited and rested her head on every place I sat, something he had never seen her do before.

In a visit filled with magical moments, this would be one of my most cherished memories. Fred believed that Kitona knew I belonged to my mother.

Chris riding Mista and sister Len

Chris with Kitona

Arriving home, one of the first things I did was contact the Adoption Agency. Armed with new information about my mother, I was determined to get the details around my birth and adoption. A new social worker took my call. After catching Linda up to speed, I explained it was time to give me all the remaining information they were holding about my mother. I explained that secrets had been revealed, and the family had survived. She retrieved my file and proceeded to read the information over the phone. I was relieved and not fully prepared as she included *all* redacted and previously hidden sections. What she revealed was heartbreaking.

"Mildred Lois was a petite sixteen-year-old when she became pregnant. There was no father's name provided. Her pregnancy didn't show until late in her term. The adoption was arranged by her mother, Agnes. She was taken from her home and sent to St. Vincent's Home for Unwed Mothers in Philadelphia, several weeks before her June due date."

I had done research about real accounts of what happened to many of these young unwed mothers in the 1950's. They were often shunned by their communities and families. It was a standard practice to hide them away to avoid damaging the family's reputation. Adding to their emotional trauma, some of the homes had strict policies prohibiting the new mothers from seeing or holding their babies. Mothers were punished for their "sins" by some of the nuns, who withheld pain medication and anesthesia. There was no specific mention in the file as to what my mother's experience had been. I choose to imagine a compassionate nun, helping her.

Another piece just fell into place from the past-life regression therapy session that I couldn't figure out. In addition to the locked metal box covered in chains, I had also seen black and white cloth dolls in the background. There had to be some connection between the nuns that took care of my mother, and the black and white doll. I couldn't wait to look up St.

Vincent's Home to see if there were archived pictures of what the nuns wore. What the social worker was able to confirm was the date Millie left the hospital. She explained that it was common practice for the mothers to stay just a few days after childbirth. They didn't want to risk the mothers changing their minds about the adoption arrangements.

"Is there a date?" I inquired.

"Yes, there is. June 10th," she replied.

Of course. She was discharged on the exact date of her wedding two years later. My two sisters and I hypothesized that June 10th had been such a difficult day, that planning her wedding and starting a new life with Fred gave her happy memories to draw upon in the future. We will never know for sure. Fred wasn't aware I existed when they were married, and she never offered an explanation of why she chose that date.

The social worker then shared a hand-written note in the margin of the page.

"Even though the mothers were forbidden to see their babies, a nurse found your mother in the middle of the night, holding you in the nursery. She named you Denise."

I was not prepared for this revelation. I needed a moment to collect myself. Did she covertly make her way to the nursery, sneaking through stairwells and hallways, or did she have an accomplice? Perhaps there was a kind, warm-hearted nun that snuck her into the nursery in the middle of the night. No matter which version was true, I knew for sure that she was strong-willed, determined and resourceful. I like to think I inherited those traits from her.

I was "delivered" to Trudy and Joe Duffy at the main convent in Camden, New Jersey, ten weeks after my birth. Curious where I had been for those ten weeks, the social worker found additional notes that indicated they kept me at the hospital, to check out a heart murmur. *I wondered if it was more of an energetic heartbreak, being left alone, without the caring touch of my mother, helping me adjust to a new and scary world?* We know so much about the importance of the mother-child connection. Throughout most of my life I avoided painful emotions until my healing journey. The feelings of unworthiness, fear and abandonment that fully surfaced; did they have their roots in St. Vincent's Home, many years ago? Even the emotional trauma Millie experienced as a young unwed mother would have some effect on me in utero. It would seem that in this lifetime, I was destined to experience and have the opportunity to move beyond abandonment, fear, sadness, and unworthiness.

My thinking has continued to involve, and I now find the Law of Polarity (every emotion has a corresponding opposite) helpful for integrating emotional experiences. The early traumas helped me develop qualities such as compassion, resilience, adaptability, strength, and perseverance. For certain, the pain along the journey awakened me to higher levels of awareness and new understandings. Embracing the spiritual teaching that "things happen for the best" and "the universe always has a plan" proved challenging. Yet, as promised by my spiritual teachers and guides, when embraced, we can experience peace amidst the chaos, and the peace that comes from living fully in the present moment. I found this quote empowering:

"Fear and belief ask the same of us … to believe in things unseen. The choice is ours."

14

UNCONVENTIONAL METHODS

*"You live on a blue planet that circles around a ball
of fire next to a moon that moves the sea,
and you don't believe in miracles?"*

—Collective Evolution

The information-seeking part of the search for my mother had come to a close. Replacing it was a new intention to find my birth father. My sister Sis thought there might be potential clues in additional photo albums still buried in some of Mom's boxes. It was another reason to return to Ohio for the Thanksgiving holiday and browse the albums together. Sis was a researcher at heart and shared my curiosity. Thanks to her, and the rest of the family, I now possessed valuable medical information and a treasure chest of family stories. Still missing was paternal medical information and my birth father's story. Sis and I made a pact that we'd find the answers together by the end of the year.

While Dave and I had been vacationing in Bar Harbor, a flier about a psychic/medium reading caught my eye. I was drawn to Reverend Michelle Love's picture, which radiated light and compassion. I picked up the last flier and tucked it away in a pocket of my backpack. With the Ohio trip top of mind, I totally forgot about the flier, until it resurfaced while packing for Thanksgiving. Something told me to hang onto her contact information, as new information might be uncovered in Mom's albums. I had no experience with mediums and wasn't sure how Reverend Love could help me. She not only became a valuable partner helping me pull the remaining pieces together, Michelle became a trusted friend and mentor.

Growing up as an only child, with two sets of aunts and uncles who had no children, meant that our holidays were very quiet. I described them to friends growing up as boring and stressful, as I became the entertainment and center of attention. Thanksgiving at my birth mother's house was the complete opposite. I lost count as the day went on, how many grandkids, great-grandkids and cousins stopped over. There were never-ending stories and lots of chaos. It was wonderful. Sis had already unearthed five full albums and it appeared our mother had a large circle of friends growing up. We jumped into the task of taking each small photo out of their corner holders and inspecting the backs, looking for names. I recorded the names of anyone that occurred multiple times to research when I returned home. The internet connections at the farm were less than ideal. My research into her school girlfriends proved a dead end. The ones that I could find had all passed on. I had hoped that even with being sworn to secrecy by her mother, maybe Mom had confided in one of them.

While looking through the last photo album, the break we were hoping for happened. There were numerous pictures of the same boy from junior high through high school. The last few pages contained multiple pictures of Mom and this boy together as teenagers. Two were particularly interesting. Mom looked to be about fifteen or sixteen. In one picture she was embracing the teenage boy, and in the second, they were locked together in a kiss. Sis's memory was triggered as she recalled stories Mom shared about a boy back in New Jersey named Robert, that she was quite fond of. Sis enthusiastically declared, "Robert is the one. He has to be your father. Look at these photos."

Call it fate or divine intervention years ago when my mother assembled the photo albums...out of the hundreds of photographs we had looked through, only *one* picture included a first *and* last name on the back. And the first name on that one photo was indeed Robert. We now had a complete name to research, Robert Butler. Sis took on the responsibility of locating Mom's first cousins. We knew from Fred and the various photos that Mom visited Kentucky each summer. Two names stood out for Sis that showed up in many of the photos, Janet and Ruth Ann. Maybe Mom confided to one of them against her mother's wishes? The entire family offered to look through their address books and old Christmas cards, to see if there were any recent addresses. It was a nice change to have a small army of detectives, helping find clues that might reveal answers about my birth father.

I left Ohio the second time, with even more appreciation for this wonderful family that had been so generous and supportive. My backpack was full of notes and copies of the relevant pictures. My scientific mind was satisfied with the plan we mapped out and the opportunity to research new facts and data. Dave reminded me about the dream I had at the beginning of my integrated journey. It had delivered a clear message about using "unconventional methods." I had thought that the medical medium and past-life progression therapy were the extent of the alternative methods needed. At the same time, I couldn't shake off the idea that the flier I had tucked away months earlier in my backpack about the psychic medium readings was about to come into play. I stumbled onto an article on the science of alchemy. Alchemy is defined as, "A seemingly magical process of transformation, creation, or combination. Taking something ordinary and turning it into something extraordinary, sometimes in a way that cannot be explained." It seemed like a perfect explanation for how my healing journey was unfolding. I was blending the scientific with the mystical to create something totally unexpected. At this point, I had no idea how extraordinary the story was about to become.

Research into Robert Butler from New Jersey and people connected with that name proved relatively easy. After eliminating lists of potential connections, there was one person on Facebook named Rita Butler that seemed the most promising. She looked to be about my age, and in the right location. I sent her a friend request, with a short note explaining my family research in very broad terms. I didn't want to scare anyone away by saying, "I'm looking for my birth father!" I asked her if she was connected to Robert, and was she willing to connect me with him. She responded quickly, saying she was an ex-daughter-in-law, and that Robert was not on Facebook. However, his wife Margaret was active on Facebook. Rita offered to connect me with Margaret. I sent a private message explaining the research I had been doing into my mother's younger years, and that Robert emerged as a close school friend. Concurrently, I set up an appointment for a reading with Reverend Michelle Love, a few weeks before the Christmas holidays. She lived in Bar Harbor, Maine during the summer months, and the reading would happen over the phone, as she was now in Florida. Honestly, I didn't understand how mediums did what they did in person, let alone remotely.

Taking a deep breath, I prepared myself for the call. I was excited and anxious to find out if she would confirm Robert as my father. Michelle explained the process that would unfold once she entered a meditative state. She did not want any background or details of why I was calling. Once she started speaking, the messages communicated were specifically for me, from across the veil. In other words, random people don't choose to make an appearance! Michelle explained that for most people the information received connected instantly and made sense. For others, the information coming through did not initially connect. Time and additional research might be needed for a complete picture to come into view, much like pieces in a jigsaw puzzle. I laughed out loud, assuring her that I was *very* familiar with that process. After several minutes of silence, Michelle began transmitting a communication.

"There is a man. Very close to you. Not your father. Possibly an uncle? He has strong arms. There is a small stone block house behind him, with a very large chimney on the front outside wall of the house. It looks like there is metal furniture on the front patio. He liked cigars, a long time ago." Before she continued, she asked me if I recognized this person?

"Yes. It's my Uncle Gus. My father died when I was in high school and Uncle Gus became a surrogate father. Uncle Gus died ten months ago, just a few months after my diagnosis. He was ninety-six. After returning home from WWII, he married my adopted mom's sister, Betty. Together, they built their small stone block house on her family's farm in South Jersey. The house does have a very large fireplace chimney on the front face. He smoked cigars until his heart attack in the early sixties. He missed them."

I explained. "You are already exceeding my expectations."
Uncle Gus was just getting started.

"He wants you to know he has tremendous love for you.
You took care of him after Betty died, and showed him how to
be independent so he could stay in his beloved house. When
he died, you were the only person with him at the hospital.
You laid down next to him and held him when he took
his last breath. He wants you to know that he is 'Eternally
grateful' for your love and easing his concerns about dying.
He's showing me that you were holding onto him when
he took his last breath. He wants you to know he crossed
peacefully." No one but Dave and Uncle Gus knew the last
moments I shared with him. Michelle certainly didn't know
them. My left brain was asking how is this even possible;
while my heart just didn't care. Tears fell as I let myself feel
Uncle Gus's loving presence.

Michelle's channeling switched messengers. "There is a
woman coming in … perhaps your mother? She has long hair
down to her waist and had trouble breathing. She suffered
from headaches, too. Until recently, she was distraught, and
overwhelmed with guilt and sadness. Is she your mother?
It's not completely clear to me."

"Yes," I whispered. "There is only one woman that fits
this description. My birth mother, Millie."

I asked Michelle if there was a way I could ease Millie's
pain. Even as a young child I understood her desire to find a
family that could offer me a better life. Michelle responded
that my mother knew I was at peace with her, and that she
had been watching over me since her passing in September.
She was proud of the life I had created, and finding the
family was something she had always wished for. It was
something she was unable to do for me when she was alive.
She's smiling at how much you looked like her when you
were both younger.

Chris high-school graduation

With zero scientific evidence to back this up, I choose to believe that my mother was behind the multiple surgery delays and paths that unfolded, leading me to her and the family. I was meant to re-ignite my search, release buried grief, sadness and loss, and heal. My healing journey was also helping my mother heal and find peace. Michelle's words jolted me back to the moment.

"If you want to see her, just know that when you go into your bedroom and look into the large mirror that sits on top of your bureau, you will be looking at her."

Two things came into my mind simultaneously. This seemed like the creepy scene out of a scary Disney movie. *And*, how did Michelle know that my mirror sat on top of the dresser, and wasn't mounted onto the wall? The unexplainable was far from over. To my surprise, Grandmother Agnes came through. There was no mistaking her by the description

Michelle provided. She wanted to apologize, not realizing the extent of the pain she caused me. Through Michelle, she explained that she believed Fred and Millie's marriage might not survive her daughter's secret. It was later confirmed that they had gone through some rough patches. I'd like to say I forgave my Grandmother in that moment; however, it took a while longer to release the resentment I carried that kept my mother and me apart. The call with Michelle had already delivered amazing information, and I assumed the session was complete. Everyone that I thought might come through had. I was ready to ask Michelle my questions about Robert and if he was my birth dad. However, the folks on the other side were not finished with me yet. Michelle began to relay pieces of additional images coming through.

"There is a young man, moderate height and build. Brown hair, brown eyes. Wearing jeans, maybe overalls. Not a suit. Surrounded by motors and a mechanic's garage. Looks like he's in his thirties. He's repeating, "There was a struggle. I couldn't hold on." He's saying he's responsible for the 'ending of a life.'"

"What," I asked, "he murdered someone?"

Michelle responded, "No. It seems like some type of accident. There is water, tall grasses, and a railroad trestle bridge in the distance."

She asked me if Louisiana or Louis meant anything to me. It did not. I told her I have a younger brother, in his mid-thirties, and he's very much alive. He also didn't match Michelle's physical description at all. I was just learning about my new family. Perhaps there were relatives in Louisiana or a distant uncle named Louis. After pausing to see if there were any more transmissions, Michelle reminded me to save everything I had written down. She assured me that pieces would come together over time, and inquired about the reason for the session.

I explained my search and reunion with my birth mother's family, and that now I was trying to identify my birth father. Family research had given me a name and I wanted to see if she could offer any clarity through her psychic abilities.

"I'm ready for his name."

"Robert Butler."

After a few moments of silence, she said, "I know you want him to be your father. I can sense your disappointment. Robert is definitely not your father. However, you will meet him, as he has valuable information for you."

I thanked her profusely still reeling about the accuracy of the things I could verify. The descriptions of my uncle, mother, and grandmother were undeniable.

I called Sis and relayed every detail. Sis responded there was nothing in our family history that matched Michelle's communication. She was unaware of any Louisiana or Louis connection. We both left the call wondering if we'd ever make sense of it all. It turned out we would have answers just a few days later.

While Christmas shopping, I received a call from an unfamiliar New Jersey number. It was Margaret Butler, Robert's wife. I quickly pulled into a parking lot, found pen and paper, and waited for her to begin. I was certain she could hear the pounding of my heart through the phone. Margaret was direct and not afraid to ruffle feathers.

"I want you to know that I immediately grabbed Robert, sat him down at the kitchen table and said, 'If you're this girl's father you need to come clean now!'"

Oh my! This poor guy is in his 70s and getting accused by his wife of having a daughter with an old girlfriend. I had been very careful not to imply anything like this in my note. Clearly, she was one step ahead of me.

I could hear Robert's voice in the background. The next thing I knew, he jumped on the line. He was also direct and funny. I felt an instant connection with him, and was hoping Michelle had been wrong about Robert not being my father.

"Honey, of course I remember your mother. She was really pretty with great legs. We used to go to the roller-skating rink. Millie loved to dance and she wore cute short skirts. I am positive I'm not your father, because we never had sex. Not because I didn't want to, believe me. I was the captain of the baseball team and in contention for a scholarship. I couldn't mess that up."

Whoa ... a little too much info about my mother's sexy skirts and great legs. And, a definitive answer from Robert that I believed. He was very interested in what I was up to and why. I explained my healing journey, recent research with Mom's photo albums, and a desire to locate my birth father. He was very willing to fill in the gaps. He explained they went to different high schools, and met at a party.

"Robert, I was born in June, 1956. Millie's birthday was the end of November. She would have been seventeen when I was born. From the pictures I've seen, Sis and I guessed you both were around sixteen."

Millie and Robert

"Robert, do you remember how old you were when you broke up? And did Millie date someone right afterward? She would have gotten pregnant around Labor Day for me to be born in early June." Robert answered quickly, with no hesitation. The break-up happened midsummer between their junior and senior year of high school.

"We were both sixteen. She started running with a guy that had a reputation for being wild and a little sketchy. A James Dean kind of tough guy that rode around town on a motorcycle in a leather jacket, white T-shirt, and shades."

I thought I detected a note of regret in his voice as he said, "I never understood what she saw in him. I lost track of her after that."

"Do you recall his name?" I asked. Of course, he did.

"Derek Hughes. He went to the same high school as your mother."

Michelle had been spot on. She had been certain Robert was not my father, and certain he would have valuable information for me. Robert didn't know anything about Derek's current whereabouts. However, he offered to call the police chief and pave the way for me. He and Robert were golfing buddies and knew everyone in town.

Margaret invited us for a visit when we were in New Jersey over the Christmas holidays. I was touched by their generous hearts and willingness to help. Saying good-bye proved hard. Robert had known my mother before her life changed dramatically.

"Robert, I'm genuinely disappointed that you are not my dad. It would have been an honor getting to know you," I said, my eyes filling with tears.

It was sad to think that for some reason, Mom broke off her relationship with this wholesome guy who genuinely cared about her for someone described as wild. I was very curious about what the facts would reveal.

The police chief proved very helpful. He remembered there were three brothers who owned a mechanic's garage just off the main road, outside of town. He thought they might still congregate with their buddies, even though the business was closed. This was great news and another pathway that seemed to reveal itself effortlessly. In a year full of research and dead ends, one thing I was learning was that if the path seemed blocked, instead of reactively trying to break through, it was a perfect time to pause, breathe and slow down. Discernment was required to determine if this was a time to paddle upstream against the current or let go and float downstream with the current. I was beginning to realize how much time I spent swimming against the current of my own life. The past year was illustrating three important messages.

1. I didn't have to work so hard.
2. I didn't have to do it alone.
3. People were willing to help when you asked them.

Unintentionally, had I taken my independence growing up as an only child to an extreme? Afraid it showed a lack of confidence and even weakness if I asked for help? I could see how I blocked the flow of expansive and solution-focused possibilities that develop through collaboration. The insights as a result of the cancer diagnosis and subsequent healing journey seemed never-ending. *Was this another nod to "everything happened for the best?"* Moving on to the next phase of research, I quickly discovered the name "Hughes" was very prevalent in Pennsville, the town where Mom grew up. There were more than thirty listed in the white pages. I found one with a first initial that matched one of the brothers the police chief remembered, "Z. Hughes." There was also an "L. Hughes". The medium had mentioned the name

Louis. Calling both numbers seemed a good place to start. L. Hughes answered, and identified himself as Louis. *This was a good sign.* I explained my reason for calling. It turned out he was ten years younger than Millie, however he was familiar with Zach Hughes. Zach was from a different Hughes family, and he thought he was closer to my mother's age. The police chief had referenced a "Z. Hughes" as potentially related to Derek. This was becoming very promising.

Time was running out if I was going to find my birth father by the end of the year. Christmas week was the following week, and I was working late every night preparing for a holiday vacation. Needing a mental break and something to eat, I took a stroll around the third-floor. I had no trouble finding tins of yummy Christmas cookies in the break room to serve as a late dinner. The impulse to call Zach's number *now* popped into my mind as I was heading back to my office. It was 7:00 pm, and I paused thinking it was too late to call. I made the call anyway. A gruff, older woman's voice answered. I said hello and introduced myself.

"Who is this? I never answer calls from people I don't know."

I was immediately intrigued. Why did she pick up the phone? Had I gotten an assist from someone on the other side, my mother perhaps?

Explaining the reason for my call, I asked if she was connected to Zach Hughes, brother of Derek. I sensed her hesitancy and her desire to hang-up the phone. Miraculously, she did not.

"Yes, Derek is my husband's older brother."

OMG. I actually found him?

"Could you please give me his number? I think he might have information about my mom that would be very helpful," I asked.

"No, he's no longer with us."

"I'm so sorry," I replied. "Was his death recent?"

Derek would be my mother's age and likely started smoking at a young age like she had.

"No. It was a long time ago."

It was at this point that the hair on the back of my neck started to tingle and chills went down both arms. Michelle's reading came to mind.

"Do you recall when he died?"

"Sometime around 1968."

Michelle had described a man in his early thirties. It wasn't that the man she described was thirty years old *now*, present time. What if he had been thirty in 1968! I quickly scribbled calculations on a sticky pad. It was how old my mother would have been in 1968.

"Did he die in a car accident?"

"No. A boating accident," her voice emotionless.

"I'm so sorry. Is there any way that I could talk with your husband? I'd like to know a little more about his brother."

Just that fast the call was over. I had crossed her line. She told me her husband wasn't home and promptly hung up the phone. Reeling from what I just heard, I pushed my chair back and compared the notes from the call with my notes from Michelle's reading. I had made a habit of keeping my journal with me for just such an occurrence.

Michelle described a young man in his early thirties in jeans or overalls. Check.

The police chief said the Hughes brothers had owned a mechanic's garage together. Michelle referenced a mechanic's garage. Check.

The death year and age matched. Check, check.

Michelle also said the young man was "responsible for the ending of a life" and a struggle. Did the boating accident involve other people, and did someone accidentally die?

The old woman described his death as an accident. Same distinction that Michelle made. Another check.

164

Michelle had told me at the beginning of the reading that random people don't just pop into her consciousness. The ones who come through are connected to the person doing the asking. Robert had identified a person and a name that just happened to die at a young age in a way that matched Michelle's transmission. Having to become my own Adoption Detective, there were many times my scientific sensibilities were challenged. By far, this was the most challenging. There were many connections discovered, yet still no definitive proof.

Google was no help, as the death happened in 1968. On my drive home I considered the reporting and recording options in 1968. A boating accident resulting in a death of a young man would have been front-page news in 1968. I learned from Robert that the town he and Mom grew up in had two high schools. They would have a decent library and possibly a historical society. When I arrived home, I verified that Pennsville had both.

I called the historical society as soon as they opened the following morning. A friendly voice answered, and indicated she had time to hear the background context for my request. She enthusiastically agreed to begin searching the microfiche for newspaper articles from 1968. It would take a few days and she promised to call with the results.

The day before Christmas Eve, Dave and I left Maine on the 7-hour drive to New Jersey to visit his family. Midway into the drive, the woman from the historical society called back. Her voice was filled with excitement.

"You were right!" she said. "It was a giant news story and front page on all the South Jersey papers. I've made copies and put it in the mail for you. You should have it in a few days."

I explained that we were in the car on our way to New Jersey, and could she read what she had sent? I couldn't wait another minute to find out the whole story. She read us her summarized findings.

"The accident happened over Fourth of July weekend, 1968. Derek had bought a new motor boat, and took his wife and three children to a tributary off the Delaware River for their first outing. It was a glorious day for their maiden voyage. They had just finished eating lunch and everyone was fishing. His youngest daughter, who was five, suddenly caught a fish. She was so excited, as she turned to show her father she lost her balance and fell into the water. Derek reached into the water to grab her, but the current was too strong and fast. He couldn't hold onto her, and she was swept away in the current. He jumped into the water and made his way toward her. Tragically, they never made it back to the boat, and both drowned."

This information was heart-wrenching. Taken alone, the deaths of both Derek and his daughter were overwhelming. Adding to the trauma was Derek's wife and her other children witnessing their deaths. What everyone in the family endured was incomprehensible.

I needed to ask the obvious next question, "Do you know the little girl's name?"

"Her name was Louanna."

Dave and I looked at each other speechless. Michelle had asked if Louisiana or Louis meant anything to me. At the time, it did not. It certainly meant something now. The little girl's name was an unmistakable match. As Michelle predicted, Robert was critical in my search. He provided Derek's name as my potential birth father. Michelle's reading brought forth a man of whom I had no previous knowledge, who would match the circumstances of Derek's untimely death. The information provided by the woman from the historical society was invaluable. I thanked her profusely and let her know we would visit a few days after Christmas and review the articles she had copied.

The next question placed me in familiar territory. How to best approach people still alive with access to medical and family history information? My mother's search revealed a family secret, my father's search involved resurrecting an unspeakable tragedy involving two deaths. After the Christmas festivities, we drove from Dave's brother's house to Pennsville, a town forty-five minutes south on the New Jersey-Delaware state line. We found the tiny bungalow where my mother grew up, and retraced her footsteps to her schools and the downtown area. It was heartwarming to walk in her footsteps, and I imagined that I was seeing through her eyes. Saving the Hughes' family garage visit for later in the morning, we stopped to get coffee and donuts to ensure they had to invite me in! Approaching the weathered door, I could see a small group of men inside, sitting across from a large oak desk. The air was hazy due to the cigarette smoke. Taking a deep breath, I pushed the door open. They must have thought I was from Mars, bursting into their Boy's Club. My Maine puffer coat was white, topped with a faux fur trim hood. I had to look ridiculous entering their greasy mechanic's garage. The oak desk was across from the entrance door, and the oversized leather chair behind it was empty. Three men sat along the opposite wall across from the desk in various upholstered chairs that had seen better days. Everyone had a coffee mug; the mood was cordial and curious. I introduced myself, offered the donuts, and asked if Mr. Zach Hughes was there. They looked at me, then each other, and in unison replied, "Nope."

They were clearly having some fun on my behalf. I could play their game too.

Smiling, I sat down in the empty chair directly across from the desk. Suddenly, the back-room door opened, and a man about six feet tall with sandy blond hair and blue eyes came forward and sat behind the desk. There was authority in the way he moved. He placed his elbows on the desk, palms and long fingers pressed together, as if he were holding court. Reintroducing myself, the man behind the desk confirmed that he was Zach, Derek's brother. I briefly explained my research and that I had discovered Millie and Derek were friends in high school.

"Zach, would you be willing to fill in some of the gaps about your brother?" I asked.

He humored me with a nod and a wink. I guessed he was in his sixties and still fancied himself as quite the lady charmer. My first question drew a very unexpected response, and helped answer one of the most perplexing question my sisters and I had about how I came to be in the world.

"Can you tell me what your brother was like?"

"Well, Derek rode a motorcycle and loved his black-leather jacket. Back then, we made moonshine in the basement. He always carried a flask in his jacket pocket. Man, that stuff was strong. One sip, and it could take you out if you weren't used to it."

My mind reeled. Wait? What did he just say? I asked a broad, open-ended question, with an infinite number of possible answers. His answer sent shivers up and down my spine. I recalled a baffling conversation with my two sisters during my second visit. We were talking about how Mom got pregnant and did they have any theories. Len and Sis talked about how once they started going out to parties, Mom sat them down and gave them the same lecture before they left the house.

"Never, ever, leave your drink unattended. If you have to go to the bathroom, give it to a friend to watch, or take it with you."

Mom never explained herself, however the girls always suspected something sinister happened when she was dating. And this was before they knew I existed. They also found it curious that as an adult, she never drank any alcohol. Sitting across from Derek's brother, I tried to show no emotion as my mind processed the peculiar fact about the moonshine.

Did Zach just tell me how I came to be in this world? Was there an end of summer Labor Day party, and my mother got drunk on the strong moonshine? Or worse, was something slipped into her drink and she was taken advantage of? I had begun to recognize body sensations like the hair rising on the back of my neck, or tingles through my body as a sign to pay very close attention to what was unfolding in the moment. My entire body felt like it was pulsating. Needing time to collect myself, I asked Zach if there were any photos of his brother in the garage office. There were none.

"Did he look like you?" I was hoping the answer was no, as the man in front of me did not resemble Michelle's physical description of Derek other than the overalls.

"Nope. He wasn't near as good looking! Brown hair, dark brown eyes, **just** like yours."

Wait, was he implying something here?

"Medium build. He was a great mechanic and worked here in the garage until his death."

The physical description matched Michelle's description. Zach offered details of the accident not mentioned in the newspapers.

"The family had just finished eating lunch when the accident happened. When Louanna fell overboard and was swept away by the current, Derek managed to catch up with her. He grabbed her by one arm, then tucking her in close, he began making his way back to the boat. The current was very strong and running against him. They had just finished eating lunch, and his wife believes because he was working so hard, he got cramps. All of a sudden, he disappeared under the surface of the water; holding Louanna tightly against his chest as they both went down. They never surfaced alive."

Tears streamed down my face. This was a tragic story, far worse than the newspaper reports. After the accident, Derek's wife returned to her childhood home in the Midwest with the two surviving children. Which meant I had two more half-siblings somewhere in the world. Given the circumstances, I had no desire to approach them. The family had been through enough. Zach's detailed description confirming Michelle's communication about a struggle, and being responsible for the ending of a life, left nothing else to uncover. Zach gave me directions to the site of the accident just a few miles up the road. Before I left, somehow, I remembered to ask about Zach and Derek's parents and grandparents. The Hughes family were English, Scottish, and Irish. The elders lived well into their nineties and died from "natural causes." There was no cancer anywhere in the family that he was aware of. I had decided earlier not to reveal the true intent of my visit, and I think he knew already. Thanking him for his time, I closed the garage shop door and made my way back to Dave, who was waiting in the car. As we left the parking lot, my appreciation for Zach and the help he offered grew. He could have asked me to leave, suspecting my real motivation for being there.

We followed Zach's directions to the site where the accident happened. It was exactly as he described. There was an old house on the big bend where the current raced by, next to a giant pine tree. This was where the bodies had washed up on shore.

Dave said, "Didn't the medium say something about tall grass and a railroad trestle bridge in the distance where the accident took place?"

Out on the horizon was a trestle bridge and we were completely surrounded with tall marsh grasses. Off in the distance, I noticed a very large bird flying toward us. Uncle Gus, who came through Michelle's transmission, always comes to mind when I see a turkey vulture flying. I couldn't make it out from the distance, if that's what this was. Uncle Gus had worked on a turkey farm as a young boy during the Depression, and told stories about the vultures that plagued the farm. He thought it was a metaphor for life: when you were close up to them on the ground they were butt ugly, yet in the sky, with distance and perspective, they were the most magnificent fliers. Not bad for a fellow who only had a sixth-grade education before they took him out of school to work on the farm. Just minutes after Uncle Gus took his last breath, I saw a turkey vulture soar across the sky outside his hospital room window. While making arrangements at the funeral home later that day, three more turkey vultures circled overhead. Uncle Gus appreciated a great sense of humor.

As this bird came closer, it was obvious from how it was soaring that it was a turkey vulture. The bird flew straight towards where we were standing, landing at the top of an old pine tree.

Before leaving Uncle Gus, the night before he died, I whispered in his ear,

"I could really use your help when you get to the other side. Lots going on, that you'll figure out when you get there." I hadn't told him about my cancer diagnosis, because he would have worried. And I definitely hadn't told him I was trying to locate my birth mother.

Standing beneath that pine tree, looking out across the water, I felt his presence and heard him say, "Here you go, Chrissy. I did what you asked me to do. Rest now, you've found what you were looking for."

We sat on the deck in silence, honoring the process and thanking the people who helped me find my birth father. I thanked Derek for my life, and sent prayers to his family.

Curious to see pictures of Derek as a healthy young man, since we were in the area we decided to still go to the historical society. I could personally thank the woman who helped and see the articles for myself. Interestingly, there were no pictures of Louanna or her father. The article contained pictures of the recovered bodies under sheets. Missing were the happy, small pictures that normally appear in the newspaper when someone dies. We went to the library, and painstakingly went page by page through the yearbooks hoping to see a picture of Derek. There were no pictures anywhere. If he did graduate, he never showed up for his cap-and-gown picture. I've come to believe that I wasn't supposed to have any images of him in my mind. And since no birth-father name was provided to the Adoption Agency, I don't think Derek ever knew Millie was pregnant. There were no pictures in Mom's photo albums with his first name, either. Likely, it was a brief encounter of some kind, not a relationship. The last stop we made before leaving New Jersey was to see Robert and his wife, Margaret. They were even more delightful in person, and we celebrated the crucial role they played in making 2010 a year to remember.

Fred and Millie would have the final word for the year 2010. Returning home to Maine, we found presents had arrived from my new family in Ohio. Fred sent a card, with a one-hundred-dollar bill, and a hand-written note.

"Dear Chrissy, Millie and I had a tradition to give each of the adult children money at Christmas time. We've missed a lot of Christmases with you. Not this year! Here is a gift from your mother and I. With love, Fred."

There would be only one more Christmas card from Fred. Emphysema took his body and freed his spirit to be with his true love, Millie.

Fred's favorite picture of Millie.
It had a forever home in his wallet.

15
TRUTH HEALS

"Afterall those years as a woman hearing 'not thin enough, not pretty enough, not smart enough, not this enough, not that enough,' almost overnight I woke up one morning and thought: I'm enough."

—Anna Quindlen

"How about a road trip to Kentucky?" Sis asked as spring approached. The upcoming summer offered a great opportunity to spend time together, visit the old homestead, and meet Mom's extended family. She shared my excitement in finding my birth father's information and we both looked forward to what we might discover in Kentucky. Neither of us thought anything could top the prior year. We could not have been more wrong. The Kentucky trip would deliver the "mother" of all revelations. The first order of business, and important to the success of the road trip, was to locate Mom's cousins and Aunt Hazel, our Grandmother's sister. No one had heard from them for a very long time and the trail had run cold. "Out of the blue" Sis received a note from Janet, one of the cousins Mom talked about. Janet found Sis's address from an old Christmas card. It was no surprise that Sis was looking for her while Janet was looking for Sis. We saw this as a sign the trip had already been blessed. A family reunion on our maternal side was scheduled in the fall, in Moorhead, Kentucky, just a few miles from the old homestead. The best news of all, Mom's cousins would be all be there, and Aunt Hazel, who was very much alive and in her eighties. I was hoping the family secret had leaked out and the last matriarch knew something we hadn't learned yet.

We would proudly represent Mom's Ohio family. I met Sis in Ohio and we drove over the winding hills of Kentucky, talking non-stop. There were a lot of years to catch up on. We had arranged to meet three of Mom's closest cousins for breakfast at the Cracker Barrel just off the highway in Moorhead. Janet had traveled the furthest, coming with her husband from Alabama. Ruth Ann lived in the area, and Joan drove in from Ohio. They were funny, wonderful women and Sis provided the cliff-note version about what had been happening since Mom died, and how I found the family.

It became clear as breakfast continued that something significant had happened years ago that caused a break between the cousins and my mother. Janet leaned in across the table and shared what had caused them such sadness.

"Lois (Mom's middle name and what the family called her in Kentucky) visited the homestead from New Jersey every summer, as a young girl and teenager. There were nine cousins, and we all got along, playing and doing chores on the farm.

Millie on the family homestead in Kentucky

Lois came with a suitcase of nice clothes and stories about school and her life in the city. Returning home, Lois's suitcase would be mostly empty, as she left behind the clothes the cousins liked best. Despite her mother's disapproval, she would repeat this practice every summer. Then something significant happened one year. School ended in June, and no Lois. She never arrived. And the following summer, the same thing. There were no letters of explanation, and the few times they could get a phone call out, they were never answered. There was no communication with the Kentucky family until they were notified of Grandad's death, in 1974.

"It was the first time we heard from Lois and Aunt Agnes in over twenty years," Janet concluded.

She had tears in her eyes just retelling the unfolding of events. Sis and I looked at each other, knowing the reason Mom never returned. Sis explained it for everyone.

"Mom gave birth to Chris in early June, 1956. It was the summer between junior and senior year. It would have been impossible for mom to travel to Kentucky that summer, and not tell all of you. Clearly, Grandmother was not going to risk the secret getting out by having mom travel in subsequent summers."

I filled in the gaps from conversations I had with Fred when he found out after Grandad's death. Their sad expressions changed to surprise as they began to pull the time-lines together. It appeared our journey to Kentucky was already bigger than a simple family reunion. This trip was about healing past ancestral wounds and allowing my family the space to know the truth and let go of the resentment and pain. One of the cousins put to words what we were all thinking.

"Lois was just a child, alone with her pain and a secret that couldn't be shared with the people closest to her. She lost her friends and the place that nourished her each summer. She used to tell us how lonely she was with her father gone most of the time, and no brothers or sisters. We had come up with a lot of reasons why she never came back to us. This revelation never made the list!"

Curious, I asked what they had come to believe.

"Aunt Agnes always had an "air" about her when she was around our mothers. It seemed after she left the farm, she thought she was better than everybody else. We just assumed Aunt Agnes corrupted our Lois, and she chose her city friends over her hillbilly cousins from Kentucky."

How sad that a misunderstanding was carried for over 50 years! It was no wonder we had been guided to make this road trip, and Janet's note had found Sis. They turned their attention to me, and wanted details of my life. We ordered another round of coffee and tea, and settled in. Sis affectionately named me the "Adoption Detective" and they were fascinated to hear about medical intuitives, psychics, and mediums. Parts of the story stretched their sensibilities, just as it had mine, initially. Yet, there comes a point where you can't dispute the results, and explaining it no longer matters. They were very curious who from the family first contacted me, guessing Steve. Sharing how generous and helpful Steve had been reminded me of the still unanswered question about possible Native Ancestry. I was hoping they might have some information for us. Janet's response had to win the grand prize! She looked over at Sis and me, perplexed by my question.

"What do you mean? There's a book about us."

"What?" we exclaimed at the same time. Everyone in the Cracker Barrel turned to see what the fuss was about.

"There is a book about our family history," she repeated.

"When you say a book, do you mean a pamphlet? Or are you saying there is a real book, with a cover and a spine?"

Laughter ensued; the cousins pleased they had the opportunity to surprise us.

"Yes, a real book, called *The Life of Henry Bare of Caney Creek, Ky.*"

Among the three of them, they recounted an incredible story of resilience and courage about our ancestors. The family tree began in Zurich, Switzerland, near the river Barens. It was believed that the surname Bear, received in the early eleven-hundreds, was derived from their proximity to the nearby river. The archives showed multiple spellings of the surname, including Baer, Bare, and Bear. I was speechless. Growing up with virtually no information about my ancestry, only to discover a book tracing our roots back to 1125, was a dream come true.

Janet explained that in the Zurich archives dating from the mid sixteen-hundreds, the authors had found the actual letter from Henry Bear asking the Elector for permission to marry. Permission was granted and they worked as indentured servants on a small parcel of land. Our more "recent" ancestors, George Peter and Catherine Bare, left their homeland for the Americas around 1753. They came with other Mennonite immigrants seeking religious freedom. They made their way to Rotterdam, and boarded the ship "Snow Rowand" for the long voyage to the New World. The ship docked on the Delaware River in Philadelphia, Pennsylvania in September, 1753. *Well, how bizarre is this? Grandad and my birth father both died on the same river that carried my ancestors to new beginnings and opportunity in America.* I added this peculiar coincidence to the growing list of synchronicities that still filled me with awe. And finally, the Native Ancestry part of the story was revealed. Our ancestors, Peter and Catherine, settled in Virginia, then Pennsylvania, eventually making it to Kentucky, just up the road from where we were staying.

Sometime in the early 1800's one of their children, Henry Bare, married Devina Keeze and they made their home in Caney Creek, Kentucky, now a coal town in Morgan County. Devina's mother, Sally, was a full-blooded Cherokee Indian. Finally, definitive proof of our Cherokee ancestry and connection. Devina was our third great-grandmother. Sis did additional research on Ancestry.com and discovered multiple women in our bloodline that were Cherokee. And even more surprising, she found Cherokee ancestors from North Carolina in Grandad's lineage as well.

Maternal great grandparents (The Bears)

I had been greatly affected as a child learning the truth about Native American tribes forced off the land they loved, their cultures crushed. And as an adult, I was unable to speak even hours after viewing the film *Dances with Wolves. It seemed I was watching my past life on the screen.* And now, I had the honor of volunteering with the International Council of 13 Indigenous Grandmothers and experiencing how my heart beats in rhythm with their sacred ceremonies, and my blood sings and dances along with the ancestors' sacred songs.

"How do we get copies of this book? Can we copy one of yours?" Sis asked.

Ruth Ann laughed. "You get it like any other book. You order it on Amazon!"

Joan had been impressed that the Cherokee people were a matriarchal society with respect for the sacredness of all beings. Various passages indicated the Cherokee taught the early settlers how to survive in the mountainous land, and a trading relationship developed between the Native peoples and the white settlers. A particular story stood out and made us all proud of our strong Cherokee lineage. Rebecca, one of Devina and Henry's children, was doing chores out in the side yard while her children were playing on the edge of the woods. She heard a commotion and saw a black bear heading toward the children. She grabbed a big stick and stood down the bear.

My mind was reeling as we headed for the family reunion. I had been really curious about the various spellings of mom's maiden name. Ruth Ann explained it had to do with survival. President Andrew Jackson and the United States government systematically removed Indigenous People from their lands. White people with mixed heritage anglicized their names, for fear of reprisals. Later that weekend, we had a chance to see for ourselves the various spellings on our ancestors' tombstones depending on the time period. It also seemed my ancestors had been playing a cosmic joke on me for years. From the first time I had seen a Zuni stone bear carving, I was infatuated with the shapes of the bears and their symbology of strength, confidence and standing against adversity. The very first piece of Native jewelry I owned was a bracelet with embedded cut stone bears. Over time, my extensive "bear" collection expanded, to include pottery and paintings. I laughed out loud.

"What's going on?" Sis asked.

"You aren't going to believe this. All those years searching for my ancestral roots, and our Bear ancestors were dropping 'bear' clues all over the place." We all agreed there are things that just can't be explained logically.

My First Stone Bear

In addition to the cousins and the book, the other highlight was meeting our great aunt Hazel. Unable to travel to the reunion, we brought the reunion to her. She lived at the end of a dirt road, in a double wide trailer, a common home in rural Kentucky. She had a porch overflowing with flower pots and ceramic critters in the front yard. It was a happy place. Aunt Hazel and her daughter were waiting for us on the porch. Aunt Hazel reminded me of Master Yoda from Star Wars, as she made her way to the car. She was tiny, deeply tan, and wrinkled in that beautiful wise-woman way. Introductions were made as she ushered us into her living room.

Word had spread that Sis was bringing a "mystery guest." I was given the seat of honor next to aunt Hazel on the couch. She sat so close to me she was almost in my lap; her arm wrapped tightly around my back as if she was afraid I was going to disappear. She looked at me and smiled.

"Tell me everything."

Sis recounted the story of what Mom had told Fred years earlier. Aunt Hazel interrupted numerous times with various questions, same theme.

"I can't believe this. How is it possible that my own sister never told me that she had a granddaughter? How could she keep such a secret from me all these years? And what about our Lois?"

She wasn't challenging the validity of what she was hearing. She was trying to make sense of it. Aunt Hazel patted my cheek, turned to face the room and proclaimed,

"If I had known our Lois was in trouble and needed our help, I would have adopted the baby and raised her here!"

Okay, not the response I had expected. I looked around the room, at the worn furnishings, and the beagle trying to get onto my lap with fleas happily racing around his belly, and realized how different my life would have been. Definitely loved and cared for, yet the trajectory would have taken a very different course. It was aunt Hazel's daughter, who provided needed relief as she boldly declared,

"No, you wouldn't. Think about what it was like back then. I remember you and the other women in the neighborhood talking about the "poor bastard" boy that lived up the road."

Aunt Hazel assured me that she would never have turned her back on her Lois. I believed her. Hugging everyone good-bye, we promised to stay in touch. We cousins continued our sightseeing tour, including the old homestead where Mom and her cousins used to play. It was a rambling white house with a porch, perched on a hill with a beautiful view of the farm land below. It seemed my mother created a life with Fred that looked remarkably similar to her favorite childhood summer place. She chose a life where she would be surrounded with animals, and lots of children and grandchildren growing up on a farm.

I ordered the book while still in Kentucky, and it was waiting for me when I returned to Maine. I discovered my own stories much like the students from my genetics class. It was the descriptions of their ancestors that triggered my search years earlier. Now I had my own stories which included ancestors who persevered and managed to thrive in a foreign land, creating partnerships with the Native American tribes. I was filled with appreciation for those who came before me, recognizing it was on their strong and resilient shoulders I stood. I was humbled and comforted knowing Sis and I played a part in helping the cousins and aunt Hazel gain closure and peace with Mom. I imagined it somehow helped her, too.

I had reached the end of my Adoption Detective assignment. What remained was scheduling the appointment with the surgeon from Massachusetts General Hospital that Peggy Huddleston had recommended. She was a supporter of the clinical data from *Prepare for Surgery, Heal Faster: A Guide of Mind-Body Techniques,* and an advocate for strong doctor-patient partnerships. Not only was she a highly-respected Gynecological Surgeon, we also shared a connection with India. Once a year, she volunteered in India, caring for women who had no access to medical care. I sensed we would be kindred spirits and knew I would be comfortable in her care. We mapped out a plan to definitively prove there was no cancer. As a result, I was able to retain all original body parts and experience a complete healing.

This scientist is a convert to believing in things unseen and the power of the body-mind-spirit connection. My health care team leveraged their expertise and wisdom and created an environment where I could heal on all levels. And my mindfulness practice of yoga and meditation taught me how to trust my intuition. Becoming deeply relaxed and focusing on outcomes, not problems, reduced the stress and anxiety that were undercurrents in my body for years.

Upon deep reflection, I have come to believe that the "cancer healed me." The diagnosis jolted me awake to the reality of how unbalanced my life had become. With considerable assistance from family, friends and healers, I was able to hit the "pause button" of my life. In the stillness, the messages and guidance received were able to be heard. Along the way, I discovered self-inquiry and honest reflection were helpful teachers not interested in destroying me! Much like the pulsation of a star that contracts before it expands, I needed to turn within to heal mind-body-spirit. As my awakening process unfolded changing every aspect of my life, new possibilities emerged expanding my horizons. I am not suggesting that people follow my path. I am suggesting that we give ourselves permission to create the space in our lives for being-ness. After all, we are human beings, not human doings. And in that space, we get to create *our* unique path to happiness and wholeness.

16

EPILOGUE

*"There is always light, if only we're brave enough to see it.
If only we're brave enough to be it."*

—Amanda Gorman

Seven years after the conclusion of my integrated healing journey, my professional career abruptly ended in January, 2018. I had just returned from a business trip to the Southwest, and upon entering my office, I discovered it occupied by the person I was reporting to at the time. This was unusual as he was never in the building on Fridays. Moments later, we were joined by our division's Human Resources representative. He was carrying a manila folder. Instantly knowing what this meant, waves of fear pulsed through my body. I fought back tears as I prepared myself for what was coming next. They told me my position had been eliminated, and my last day would be in two weeks. Having had to eliminate positions myself over the course of my career due to budget constraints or an individual's poor performance, this was different. I was close to celebrating my twentieth anniversary, and had the honor of accumulating numerous awards and accolades during my career. This felt like a betrayal and an ambush.

With two weeks to finish projects, I had to pack an office that was a second home to me, and say good-bye to incredible people. So many of the people to whom I said good-bye had supported me through my adoption search and healing journey. They were more than colleagues; they were friends and my second family. It was a struggle to stay in the present moment, and not succumb to the fear and anxiety about the future.

I walked out of the building for the last time on my adopted mothers' birthday, February 2. Was she trying to tell me something? She always worried about the extensive travel and hours that I worked. Was it possible this was a blessing in disguise? Once I got to my car, I took inventory of the hundreds of times I had taken this journey home, and what my career meant to me. In the moment, it felt like the furthest thing from a blessing.

Professionally, I had no idea what to do next. My husband had retired a year earlier and I was the income -generator. Close to turning 62, it was a forced early retirement that I wasn't prepared for and didn't want. Dave and I needed to make some very important financial decisions about our future. Our house in Maine, with vast gardens and glass art that Dave had created, was a special place which friends referred to as their sanctuary. There was no doubt it had been my sanctuary, and the thought of leaving it compounded my sadness. We discussed two obvious scenarios. One, stay in Maine and start over again in another company. Second, move to an economically friendly state, and take some time to sort things out. Starting over in New England just didn't feel right. Something about it felt like a step backward, emotionally and spiritually. Another possibility presented itself...maybe it was time to close a beloved chapter and begin a new one. And the universe decided I needed a push. Now it was time to rise above my fear of the unknown and see the possibilities. How to do this when my heart was breaking was the *real* question.

I turned to a trusted astrologer for insight into the bigger life themes unfolding. Margaret stated that based on the planetary alignments at my birth and where they were currently stationed, it was time to leave my old life behind and start anew. Instead of feeling joy and optimism about future possibilities, all I could do was allow the tears of sadness to pour out of me.

"Margaret, I hear what you are saying. However, I loved my old life. I'm not interested in a new one. This was not part of the plan I mapped out for this time in my life."

I recognized that I was simultaneously in the emotional upset, while also detached and observing it. On one hand, it seemed like I was falling apart. On the other hand, there was a deep calm, and an inner knowing that I was up to the challenge and would be ok. Things I had learned during another crisis in my life were about to be tested in new ways!

Somehow these fears and worries felt more intense than what I experienced during my health crisis. This felt more personal, as the identity I maintained throughout my professional career was stripped away. Concerns about my financial stability triggered sensations of fear in my body. A new layer of abandonment and unworthiness surfaced and I couldn't recall another time where I felt this vulnerable. I was an accomplished and savvy business woman who understood corporate dynamics. I knew what it took to survive and thrive in a male-dominated culture. However, for the first time, I couldn't do anything about the political decision that shifted the balance of power and left me on the outside. Much like when I came into the world, initially rejected and abandoned. Here was another chance to heal this core wound and support the inner child who had so clearly needed acceptance and security.

My dear friend and fellow spiritual seeker, Susanne, reminded me that our journey of awakening to higher levels of conscious awareness is never a straight line. Rather, it is an upward spiral where opportunities for self-growth and expansion come back around when we're strong enough to travel further. Another reminder that this new version of an old wound was not an obstacle to my path, but the very path itself.

We eventually chose to leave Maine and relocate to Florida for the financial benefits. The resulting upheaval all-encompassing, as I left my beloved home, mountains, and ocean with her rocky shoreline that always renewed my spirit, dear friends and former colleagues. Ignoring advice from the many books I read regarding "starting over," which recommended doing "nothing" for a while, I put plans in place to start a consulting coaching business and recommitted to a health and fitness regimen. I wrapped myself in a comfortable security blanket called busyness. Upon reflection, having a plan and a schedule was not just about keeping busy. For me, it also provided a sense of normalcy and certainty, important conditions for staying out of fear and rebuilding my life. My nervous system eventually calmed down and new insights emerged allowing me to focus on solutions, *not* problems and drama.

Along the way, something unexpected happened. I met an amazing community of women from different parts of the country that lived in our community. While working, I had very few friends outside of the office and was not used to just hanging out for the fun of it. My new friends were supportive, nurturing, and exactly what I needed to recharge and relearn who I was outside of a title. Before meeting this community of women, fun had been solving problems, creating meaningful learning programs and positively impacting the business. I hadn't realized how different my life had been as a corporate woman with no children. The most humorous difference came to light when a party was scheduled. Everyone excitedly talked about what they were going to cook. Hard to admit, and probably harder to believe, in forty years of marriage I had not turned on the oven or cooked a dinner. It seemed my work life had always consisted of either lots of travel, or advanced degrees and new coaching certifications. Cooking was non-existent on my priority list. Ever resourceful, I found the perfect solution for the party…no-bake, chocolate coconut, gluten-free cookies. My record remained intact!

Our time in the community was short. Florida was not what we had hoped it would be. The heat and humidity were relentless and we underestimated how much we would miss hiking and four seasons. Nine months to the day we arrived, we left Florida for Sedona, Arizona. It was the place friends and family had expected us to end up all along. It had taken nine months to "birth" a new plan and explore who I was in the word without a career. With Dave's help, the support of a wonderful coaching community from the Neuroleadership Institute, friends and my new Zumba/Yoga buddies, the ball was in my court to create infinite possibilities.

We purchased a cozy Santa Fe style house at the base of Ancestor Hill, complete with an un-restored twenty room stone Sinagua village on top. The land had been farmed by Hopi Ancestors, and our Native art finally found its right home. Fortunately, we already had wonderful friends in the area who softened our second transition. And I had come full circle in so many ways. One of our Arizona friends, June, an amazing intuitive massage therapist and healer, had brought me to this area and created a healing journey to Hopi Lands in Northern Arizona ten years earlier. We met Beth and Ross through a mutual friend who suggested we stay in their beautiful apartment on Oak Creek, complete with a direct view of Cathedral Rock, considered one of the world's most powerful vortexes. The energized area became a catalyst for writing this book. Just before my birthday, June connected me with a young Navajo/Cherokee Medicine Woman named Songbird Grandmother. She offered traditional Native birthday and healing ceremonies. I was excited for the opportunity to start my new birth year in the Southwest with Cherokee healing rituals and songs. It seemed my native ancestors were already working their magic. Before Songbird started the birthday ceremony, I shared the birthday present I had received earlier that morning. My dear friends from Florida had called and collectively sang Happy Birthday. While not a big deal for most people, for me, this had great significance. As an adopted person, surrounded by missing pieces about the circumstances of my adoption, birthdays were quiet days of reflection and offering prayers to my birth mother. Therefore, I made sure no one had sung Happy Birthday to me since I was a child. This year was a very different experience. As they sang, I felt enveloped in their collective well wishes, and my heart filled with joy and gratitude. I knew a very old story was done being told.

Songbird began the ceremony, and handed me her last gift bundle from the fire ceremonies she had conducted throughout the spring. The beautifully wrapped bag contained sacred herbs, ash from the fires, salt, and a small card. I removed the card, and found the word "HOME" printed upon it. I paused as the significance of this simple word took root in my heart. We had just moved to the Southwest, and were in the process of establishing a new life in a new home. The card also reminded me of my first visit to the Ashram, when an inner voice repeated, "You've come home." Holding the card in my hand I realized how far I had come from the idealist volunteer in Chicago, looking to find God and save the world. I truly had come home. Home to my true self, my divine essence and inherent worthiness.

The cancer diagnosis sent me on a spiritual quest and transformational journey. Breakthroughs came from the help of others, many of whom were strangers. Their compassion and support helped piece together my adoption puzzle, and gave me a story and a lineage to connect with. Beyond that was the recognition that each person along the way helped me piece myself back together. As a result, I re-discovered a profound truth: the heart is our true home and final resting place where true peace resides. Apparently, I had been the lead in a cosmic play, acting out a divine script that was more perfect than anything I could have written.

Thank you to the village of people who supported me and continue to support me through this amazing life journey. You know who you are. I honor and love each and every one of you for the part you have played in helping me *be here now*.

I offer this book with love to the community of readers who will be drawn to it. If you enjoy it, please feel free to post a review on Amazon.com to share the message. My hope is that it fills you with appreciation for *your* unique path and the realization that healing is not about fixing anything that's broken. It's about self-acceptance and remembering the peace and wholeness that is you.

With great love, with great respect,

Chris

AFTERWORD

I am honored to share the closing words of the story with my mentor and sister, Grandmother Mona Polacca, of The International Council of 13 Indigenous Grandmothers. Hopi/Havasupai/Tewa.

I met Grandmother Mona while traveling on a business trip. My friend June mentioned Grandmother Mona was speaking about the Grandmother's work that evening in Prescott, about a 90-minute drive north of Phoenix. I felt an unexplainable connection and knew I needed to meet her. I was nearing the "end" of my healing journey and struggling with how to integrate all the experiences.

I don't recall specifics from her talk. I do remember how I felt. It was as if I had come home and was in the presence of a long-lost sister. Her ancestral stories were riveting, and her healing presence communicated peace, compassion and sovereignty. That night, I began to understood the depth of what happened to Indigenous Cultures all over the world, as families literally had their children ripped from their arms, lost to them forever. The children, separated from their language, customs and culture that would never be replicated.

My hope for the future is an enlightened world that sees all children as precious divine beings to be nurtured and cared for with love, respect and dignity.

FROM GRANDMOTHER MONA:

"This is a story about the lives of the many children who grew up and children now growing up as adoptees. The challenges of one whose voice resonates with the right to know who her parents are and the bloodlines from which she comes from and the importance of acknowledging her sense of identity. Chris shares her story as part of her healing journey in such a way that anyone who reads this book can relate to their own life experience.

I applaud Chris Duffy-Wentzel for bravely facing the barriers as she walked the maze of seeking her family identity and putting the puzzle together in-spite of the many barriers she faced. She persevered and has come out finding her sense of balance so she can look to the future feeling rooted so she can have a joyful outlook towards the future.

For me it brings to mind the need for change in the old adoption laws of sealing records and not allowing the disclosure of who the parents are for the protection of the parents and not allowing even the child who has aged into adulthood to have access to such vital information related to historical family health. Such knowledge is key to adoptees in aiding in improving the quality of life and overall wellness."

—Grandmother Mona Polacca, of The International Council of 13 Indigenous Grandmothers. Hopi/Havasupai/Tewa Featured in the books: *For the Next 7 Generations and Grandmothers Wisdom: Reverence for All Creation.*

For additional information or to make a donation to support their global movement for peace, protecting our environment and human rights visit: www.grandmotherscouncil.org

ACKNOWLEDGMENTS

In the process of writing this book, I have come to realize the full meaning of the phrase "*it takes a village.*"

Ten years ago, the initial village consisted of my work colleagues who held me up while I went through my healing journey. They enabled me to let go of the reins and focus my energies on self-healing. When that part of the journey was over, their collective voices encouraged me to share my story so others could benefit. Jack, Scott, Linda and Ginny, thank you for words of encouragement and continued support. Pam and Jack C., you brought a compassionate kindness to our organization just when I needed it the most. It was an honor to "be the change we wished to see in the world." The acquisition brought together a new village. Michael, Bill, Jeff, Brandon, Joyce, Kristi and Kim, you made me laugh and lifted me up at all the crucial moments.

A special thank you to the three musketeers, who always had my back, Maureen, Deb and Laura. While we're no longer working together, I appreciate the deep connection that continues to bind us. Your encouragement and sometimes brutal, yet on-point editing suggestions are a major reason this book exists. I am in awe of the lives you are creating and so happy to still be a part of them.

Six years after what I thought was the *end* of my healing journey, I met a talented author and music therapist, Beth Kingsley Hawkins, through an introduction from a New Hampshire massage therapist friend, Jan. Beth and I met during my annual renew & recharge trip to Sedona, Arizona. It had become a spiritual oasis where I could breathe the clean mountain air, and connect with the powerful red rocks of Kachina Woman among the ancient juniper trees. Beth expressed genuine interest in my story and guided me in a music healing session, helping me get out of my mind and into my heart space. I promised her that "someday, when I stopped working" I would write my story. Which happened much sooner than I expected.

The spark was re-ignited by a new village of women from a wonderful place called Fiddlers Creek, in Naples, Florida. After unexpectedly leaving my career, friends, and home on the seacoast of Maine, they reminded me that I was now free to inhabit my own life in my own way. It was a gentle reminder that we are human "beings not doings." My heartfelt appreciation to Darlene, Marjorie, Sheri, Yolande, Patti, Ginny, Maricely, Marion, Margaret, Diane, Suzy, Lynn, Sylvie and Martine, for bringing me back to life and discovering the sheer joy of fun, laugher, community, yoga and dancing. Darlene's innocent comment that my story would help others reminded me of the promise that I had made to Beth two years earlier.

I had no idea how to begin. However, the universe definitely had a plan. Through a coaching program, I met a wonderful personal coach, Kate Lee. During one of our sessions, she asked the question that tipped the first domino.

"What small steps could you take to begin exploring writing a book?"

She expertly kept me on track for the vision I articulated. Masterfully done, Kate! And to Maria, fellow coach and traveler, you offered encouragement to leave no stone unturned in my exploration.

A very special shout-out to Ed and Mary Jones, whose expert consulting helped the sales training and development team in Boston reach new levels of excellence. And as "luck" would have it, they lived in Naples when Dave and I arrived. Your friendship provided a touchstone of familiarity and support as I started a new life in Florida.

Another "support coincidence" appeared as the medium who had provided invaluable clues about my birth family wintered in Naples. I was able to meet Michelle Love "in-person" and a fast friendship developed. Michelle, your ability to connect to loved ones on the other side in a compassionate and accurate way not only solved the rest of my adoption puzzle, you helped heal my ancestral lineage. Our deepest appreciation for you.

From Florida, the village expanded north to Tennessee, as I reconnected with a cherished friend I hadn't spoken with in years. Susanne Bennett, a transformational catalyst for me and countless others as a mentor, coach and teacher, suggested I participate in a writing workshop. Susanne has been my guide on the side throughout this writing journey, ensuring my authentic voice and feelings are breathed into every word of this heart endeavor. Namaste, my enlightened friend.

Of course, Tom Bird's Writing Workshop *happened* to be in Sedona, Arizona, at the exact place and time of a planned vacation. Tom's expertise guided me to find the "divine author within." Through his workshops, I met a supportive team of authors who encouraged and propelled me through the birthing process. Thank you, Laura, Debra and Julie, for your candor, crazy humor and open hearts. And to Tom's team, Donna, Janelle, and Arnell, thank you for your patience as you guided me through the publishing maze. Mahalo, Maui

Bill, you gave me confidence at just the right time. Ernie, thank you for diagnosing my "comma addiction" and for nurturing my story. Denise, you helped me get "over the finish line" and to soar beyond my wildest dreams.

With Tom's vast network, the village spread to New Mexico as I had the great good fortune to connect with a force of nature, Kristen White. A visionary with infinite ideas, Kristen gave me the courage to go deeper into the wounded and sacred feminine themes I had been avoiding. Through Kristen, I met a talented web designer in the Northwest, Marcus Badgley, who somehow brought my fuzzy ideas into focus with clarity and splendor.

New England villages have a reputation for being cold and aloof. This was not my experience. Two very special women nurtured me for 33 years. They knew me before, during and after my cancer healing journey. Kathy and Kelly, I'm forever grateful that your skill and talents evolved into deep friendships. Kathy, massage therapist extraordinaire, your healing touch healed my body and soothed my soul. Kelly, the person that knows my hair better than anyone, as well as every high and low of my life, thank you for still caring and checking in across the miles. And yes, if there is a screenplay, you would have a significant role!

Told by the medical medium to lose weight to save my life, I peered through the darkened glass doors at Jubilation Dance/Fitness studio with curiosity. Ten years later and many pounds lighter and stronger, thank you Honore for your courage to open the studio. And to your amazing instructors, Michelle, Leah, Maddie and Jen, you all helped me discover my inner dancer as I danced my way back to health and vitality. And who knew it would be so much fun! To the peeps I shared the floor with: Karen, Marianne, Paula, Jeri, Erin, Allison and Deb, my sister from another mother...a wild and crazy WOOO HOOOO!

And to the newest New Hampshire and Maine support team that were there when I found myself suddenly untethered and without purpose in February 2018, you were the glue that helped hold the pieces together. Much love to Karen, Jan, Lisa, Priscilla, Amee, Jeri and sweet Maddie.

These next villages are so critical that there would be no healing story to tell without their incredible expertise, love and commitment.

Dr. D'Adamo and his staff showed me what was possible outside conventional healing pathways twenty years ago, as I watched Dave self-heal without pharmaceuticals, as his arthritis reversed itself. A special shout out to MJ, best colonic nurse on the planet. You got the old stuff out and put in the good stuff. Your infectious laugh, unique humor and entertaining stories from your grandchildren helped me heal from the inside out.

Drs. Beth Devlin and George Savastio and the staff at Elemental Medicine, who believed in and supported my integrated healing journey, you provided the expert guidance and treatment that allowed me to trust my emerging intuitive self.

Peggy Huddleston, I am forever indebted to you and your life work. I'm very appreciative of *how* you wrote your book *Prepare for Surgery, Heal Faster: A Guide to Mind-Body Techniques*. The clinical data appealed to my scientific mind, and the inclusion of patient stories helped me visualize and integrate what was possible. The combination supported my healing journey *and* solved my life-long adoption mystery.

Dr. Laura Moore, there are no words that will ever adequately communicate the impact you have had on my life. From the first time we met at IDEXX, there was a deep connection beyond a business partnership. The fact that you finished Naturopathic School and returned back to the Seacoast just as I was starting my integrated healing journey can only be described as **divine intervention**. Our roots are deep and intertwined.

And for my newly discovered birth family, who opened their arms to welcome me: Thank you for your generous hearts. I never knew the depth of the heartbreak I carried until you helped me put the pieces back together. My hope is that you find this book an honoring of Mom's life that gives her the voice she wasn't able to express when she was alive. I felt her presence many times, as my fingers struggled to capture her words as fast as they were flowing in. Many blessings and much love to each of you.

Being an only adopted child with aunts that never had children meant the family that raised me was very small. They have all passed on, and I offer this book to them with appreciation for the life they gave me. Especially Trudy and Joe, who chose *and* decided to keep me! Thank you, Aunt Footsie, my best friend and inspirational role model. And to Uncle Gus, thank you for the life lessons you generously shared with us. First, a person is never too old to try new things and meet new people, which you demonstrated right up to your passing at 96. And, keep your worn and uncomfortable easy chair…it's a great way to ensure you get up and keep moving!

While my mother and father-in-law are now on the other side, Marie's loving support was present throughout this process. A sincere thank-you to my sister-in-law and brother-in-law, Bill and Mona, and their wonderful family, Adam, Kate, Damian and Kim. Your encouragement and outrageous posts keep me from taking myself too seriously!

Sedona spread her loving arms wide as I've made the Red Rock country my new home. Special thanks to the amazing vibrant Zumba community at the Cottonwood Rec Center and Pulse Pilates, who helped me find a new place to dance, laugh and sing. Grandmother Mona Polacca, June and

Songbird Grandmother, you helped me connect to my Native roots and enabled a very deep level of healing transformation. Beth, Syd, Wendy, Linda, Ashley, Candace, Angel, Karen and Kathy, thank you for your healing gifts which continue to strengthen and nurture me, body-mind-spirit. Diane, Teri, Lys, Taz and Oliver, at Twice Nice, you make me smile and laugh every Monday. Diane, your love of books and engaging stories provided an enriching environment for me to explore ideas with you. Many thanks.

It was an unexpected delight to discover a vibrant Siddha Yoga community in the Village of Oak Creek, here in Sedona, Arizona. Much appreciation to Teri, Bob, Achala, Paul, Ganga and Margaret for the spiritual centering and wellspring that always nourishes. And to Gurumayi, whose grace and teachings have sustained me through the darkest of times when all I could do was focus on one breath at a time. Siddha Yoga enabled me to transcend my fears and come home to my true self and divine essence. Many blessings and love.

And finally, to my most loyal supporter, my husband Dave. Can you ever properly acknowledge and appreciate the person that has been in your life since you were 14? Thank you dear-heart for the countless times I interrupted what you were doing to "run a word, phrase or chapter past you." Far too many to enumerate. The depth of your understanding for the meaning and purpose of our human lives, and how you have come to anchor a steady wisdom that radiates from your being, is a gift for everyone that meets you. I am forever in awe of your journey and grateful that you've chosen to share it with me. May our next chapters, as we travel and enjoy our time together, be filled with an abundance of laughter, new adventures, vitality and peace.

In closing, may the grace of our interconnected hearts from the villages we inhabit, grow stronger every day in their resolve to bring compassion, dignity, love and respect to every heart on this magnificent planet.

All my love,

Chris

ABOUT THE AUTHOR

Chris Duffy-Wentzel is a personal coach, author and speaker living in the Sedona area. Chris is certified as a Results Coach through the Neuroleadership Institute and accredited by the International Coaching Federation. Her private practice focuses on well-being and helping individuals manage careers, relationships and life transitions.

The author's transformational self-healing journey propelled her to be trained and certified by Peggy Huddleston, the author of *Prepare for Surgery, Heal Faster: A Guide of Mind-Body Techniques.* Individuals facing surgery learn how to reduce anxiety and feel peaceful before surgery which strengthens their immune system, improving outcomes.

Tapping into the creative healing energies of Sedona, Chris is committed to assisting people in creating their own unique path to wholeness: body-mind-spirit, with personal curated healing retreats. For more information please visit: kachinawoman.com

A portion of the proceeds from book sales are offered to **"Crossing Worlds Hopi Projects,"** a volunteer organization supporting Hopi sustainability, self-empowerment and cross-cultural learning opportunities. To learn more about current projects, please visit: www.crossingworlds.org

27953994R10125